CARING

Home Treatment For The Emotionally Disturbed

by

Fredric Neuman M.D.

TURNSTONE PRESS LIMITED
Wellingborough, Northamptonshire

First published in the USA by THE DIAL PRESS, New York 10017

First published in the UK by TURNSTONE PRESS LIMITED 1982

British Library Cataloguing in Publication Data

Neuman, Fredric
    Caring: home treatment for the emotionally
    disturbed.
    1. Mentally ill—Care and treatment
    2. Mentally ill—Home care
    I. Title
    649'.8   RC480.5

    ISBN 0-85500-168-2

Printed in Great Britain by
Nene Litho, Earls Barton, Northamptonshire,
and bound by Weatherby Woolnough,
Wellingborough, Northamptonshire.

CARING

A distinguished American doctor and psychiatrist
looks at how emotional and mental illness can be
treated in the home environment.

CONTENTS

FOREWORD

To the ordinary man and woman in Britain mental illness and its treatment remains difficult and confusing. In writing a guide to the subject for the general public Dr Neuman is clearly seeking to open the way to more understanding in order that unnecessary fears may be dispelled. He discusses crisis intervention in violent behaviour, child abuse, suicide and death, and the medical treatment, aftercare, prognosis and remission in a variety of mental illnesses. He does so by drawing upon his clearly considerable experience in America and illustrates the various syndromes of mental and emotional illness by well-described individual case histories. The result might be described as the intelligent lay person's guide to psychiatric illness, with particular emphasis on the role of the families involved.

Margaret Torrie, M.B.E.

CARING

A NOTE TO THE READER

A psychiatrist who has reported a case in the medical literature often has the experience of a number of his patients each claiming to be that person. We recognize ourselves, apparently, in any accurate description of other people, for all of us share to a varying degree the same virtues and weaknesses, and disabilities. It is comforting to know that our problems are not peculiar to us; but surely it is not comforting for a patient to think that a confidential account he has given of himself is spread out widely for other people to read. For that reason the readers of this book should know that no unsuspecting person appears in these pages described fully and exactly as he is in real life. The case histories in this book are summaries and composites of different people. They are drawn, a fragment here and there, not only from my own practice, but from the many patients who have come to my attention through the supervision of others. Unimportant but identifying details have been left out; others have been added. In those instances where the change of details would have blurred an accurate portrayal of a particular condition, the affected person has been described with no equivocation—but with his prior consent.

THE treatment offered someone depends on the sort of problems that he has and the sort of person that he is. Of course, in a way all people are basically the same. They share the principal experiences of life: working, playing, making love, growing up, growing old. They struggle some and suffer some, and they are joyful sometimes. They have all these things in common. And yet in another way they are all different from each other. Each person begins life genetically distinct, different from everyone else who has ever lived. He grows up into a distinctive family constellation that is different even from that of his brothers and sisters, for he is born into it at a different time. His path through life, however conventional, is different in all of its details from that of everyone else. And so, although in a way everyone is alike, in another way everyone is unique.

It is the sameness of human beings that justifies this book, for people are similar to each other also when they are mentally ill. People who are depressed or schizophrenic, or who suffer from any other type of emotional disorder, show regularities in their behavior and similarities in their state of mind. For that reason general principles or rules can be drawn up that govern the treatment of each of these conditions and that apply to one depressed person as well as to another, and to one schizophrenic as well as to another. These chapters are an exposition of those rules. But because no two people are exactly alike, even if they are suffering from the same mental illness, nothing written here should be taken as a prescription for a particular patient. *No general rules of patient care, however well drawn, can substitute for a proper evaluation by a trained person who takes into consideration the specific circumstances of his patient's life and illness and his particular distinctiveness as a human being.*

INTRODUCTION

THE number of people living as patients in psychiatric hospitals has declined over the last twenty years by more than one half, partly as the result of new antipsychotic drugs and partly as the result of new attitudes toward the mentally ill. Unfortunately these 300,000 patients have not returned to the community and to their homes entirely cured. They have symptoms still, as do the far greater number of people who have never been in a mental hospital but who are emotionally disturbed nevertheless. Indeed, emotional and mental illnesses are no less common now than they ever were. Very many people suffer transient emotional disturbances, and there are many whose disturbances are prolonged and profound. Even when these conditions are not severe, however, the people affected are unhappy and impaired in functioning. Even though they live at home, the way they live is unsatisfactory to them and difficult for everyone around them, especially for their families. And they do not grow less miserable simply by growing older. They need treatment to get better.

The burden of treatment for these troubled individuals, therefore, does not rest in the hands of hospital personnel, if ever it did. Psychotherapy in some form or another is conducted now within the community by professionals and paraprofessionals drawn from dozens of different occupations and disciplines, including—besides psychiatrists and psychologists—social workers, family doctors, visiting home nurses, welfare workers, homemakers, probation officers, divorce lawyers, drug counselors, school counselors, marriage counselors, occupational and recreational therapists, industrial counselors, and ministers and other pastoral counselors, and many others. These various professionals come in contact with the emotionally disturbed person in various ways; but in trying to help him, they must accomplish the same purposes. They try to relieve his emotional distress, and they try to help him to avoid the ineffective and inappropriate behaviors that are a characteristic manifestation of emotional illness. To do either or both, they must have some understanding of the nature of emotional illness and of the process of psychotherapy. They must understand, first of all, that by virtue of their work, *they cannot avoid doing psychotherapy.* It is inherent in any relationship in which one person turns to another for help. It is part of the process of caring. Therefore they must learn to do it as well as they can. The influence of these collateral therapists is significant. By their efforts they can change the course of an emotional illness and, thereby, the course of someone's life.

But the greatest influence on someone who is emotionally disturbed is exerted, unmistakably, by his family. They are with him every day of his life. They know better than anyone else what he is thinking and feeling and doing, and more than anyone else, they care about him. Unfortunately the complications and rivalries of family life interfere with their ability to help him. Their judgment becomes clouded; through their actions they may worsen his condition rather than improve it. Sometimes, indeed, they are the inadvertent cause for his emotional problems; but even then they can learn to behave differently for his sake. In a way they too are his therapists. They must try to help him, for they are his principal resource. Psychotherapy is not so much a precise technique as it is an attitude, a way of being with a patient; and it can be learned. But unfortunately few people are in a position to turn to a professional for supervision and instruction. Consequently, in doing therapy, they must struggle not only with the patient's problems, and indeed with the patient himself, but also with their own sense of inadequacy. This book is written to be helpful to them. It is intended as a straightforward exposition of the principles of supportive psychotherapy, as they apply to the variety of emotional and mental disorders. It cannot substitute for years of clinical experience, but perhaps it will serve as a guide to those who must care for an emotionally disturbed person and who have no other guide to follow.

1 THE NATURE AND ORIGINS OF MENTAL ILLNESS

THE concept of physical illness is readily understood: the body becomes infected or inflamed, or grows abnormally, or is affected in any number of ways, all of which can be studied conventionally with laboratory tests or under a microscope. But a mental illness is something else altogether. Mental illnesses, or emotional illnesses, are disturbances of behavior and of feeling and thought. They are disorders of function that do not correspond readily to precise physical impairments and that seem, therefore, intangible—vague, aberrant expressions of the mind. At the same time, they are elusive, because they seem to be only exaggerations of the way ordinary people think and behave. And so they are. Every person is distinctive, a particular individual with his own ideas and his own ways of doing things. The mentally ill seem special only in that they are more distinctive. They are idiosyncratic or eccentric, even peculiar; yet in their strangeness there is nothing unrecognizable. They experience no impulse nor longing that is foreign to a normal person, and they suffer

7

no illusion that a normal person has not known. The symptoms of mental illness are embedded in, and grow out of, the normal personality. Since life is varied and complex anyway, it is hard to determine where normal behavior leaves off and abnormal behavior begins. In retreat from this tantalizing ambiguity, some psychiatrists have chosen to take the position that there is no such thing as mental illness. In similar argument, one might contend that since orange blends closely into red, there is no such thing as orange.

A medical student assigned to a psychiatric ward evaluated his first patient, an eighteen-year-old girl who had been admitted to the hospital because her mother had complained that there was something the matter with her. Following an argument with a teacher, the girl had become withdrawn and preoccupied with religion. She began eating poorly and leaving her room in a mess, which was out of character, for she was usually very neat. Then on the day before her admission she was found sitting on a subway platform, dangling her feet over the edge.

The medical student, after speaking to her on a few occasions, told the director of the ward that in his opinion she was not really ill. All he noticed about her was a kind of flightiness of thought and a somewhat depressed mood, which he thought was not out of keeping with the unpleasant circumstances of being on a psychiatric ward, especially for a sensitive young girl. Although his patient had little to say about the episode in the subway station, he explained it as an adolescent prank. Adolescence is a time when one is given to silly and impulsive behavior, he said, and to preoccupations with religion, for that matter. He went on to say that there was a time during his own adolescence when he himself was concerned with religious questions. And as for messiness, his room was even now, a mess. He said in conclusion that if she was emotionally sick, he thought that perhaps he himself, and certainly some of his classmates, were sick also.

This student felt an obvious rapport with his patient which allowed him to see the world through her eyes, a sympathy that is surely at the heart of what a therapist should feel for a patient. Nevertheless he was wrong about her. The flightiness of thought that he remarked upon was the outward sign of a thought disorder; and her mood was not depressed so much as it was dulled or detached, which was a sign of a serious disturbance of feeling. Neither did her actions on the train station represent an adolescent prank, but rather the poor and, in this case, potentially dangerous judgment of an acute psychotic process; for she was indeed psychotic. The medical student was mistaken because he was not yet accustomed to looking at people clinically, which means distinguishing those particular behaviors that have significance to a person's emotional life. He couldn't tell where normal behavior came to an end and something else began. He had not yet seen orange and red set up against each other often enough to tell one from the other. As for his classmates—it is likely that he was right and that among them there were a few who were indeed mentally ill, for emotional disturbances are common, and no one is immune.

How then does a medical student or a psychiatrist—or anyone else, for that matter—decide whether a particular person is mentally ill? How, for instance, does one tell a normal adolescent from a sick one? It is quite true, after all, that all adolescents are inclined to be messy and withdrawn from time to time. The next moment they are just as likely to be obsessively clean and compulsively gregarious. They may be sexually seductive, even obscene, one moment, and ascetic the next. They live, apparently comfortably, shifting between various extremes of existence, any of which in an older person would suggest the presence of an emotional disorder. Even the sudden shifts themselves would probably be considered pathological in an adult. So the criteria for illness vary, for one thing, with age.

But consider also these other examples and decide if the particular person is normal or abnormal:

A twenty-eight-year-old woman returned home after giving birth to her first child, a girl. She and her husband had been married for eight years before they were able to conceive, and so, naturally, she was pleased when she discovered that at last she was pregnant. She said afterward that she felt happy throughout her entire pregnancy and fulfilled in a special way. Only at the very end, perhaps, was she somewhat uneasy. It came as a surprise to her, then, after she returned home with the baby, to realize that she felt let down a little. She was irritable and had trouble sleeping, even beyond what one might expect as a result of a new baby waking her up every few hours during the night. She was glad to get away from the baby for a while, and once or twice, unmistakably, she felt sad.

How should one regard her state of mind? At least to some degree she was feeling unhappy in circumstances where one would expect her to have felt quite the reverse; does that mean that she was ill? Certainly many women who have borne children have felt just as she did. Is that relevant? Because her reaction is common, does that mean that it was normal? Suppose instead of feeling sad once or twice, she felt sad all the time and was, in addition, troubled by the thought that she might drop the baby or inadvertently stab it with a pin or a scissors. Should she then be considered emotionally disturbed, or would she still be within the limits of normal? Suppose she felt so sad that she entertained the idea of killing herself? Probably then, by almost anyone's standard, she would be unequivocally emotionally ill. But suppose it was only a vague thought of killing herself, and suppose it only passed fleetingly through her mind.

A forty-six-year-old woman was experiencing those alterations in life that often characterize that age. She watched with some anxiety, and with pride, while her two daughters married and moved away; she tried to adjust to the constant presence of her husband, who had retired from the postal service and begun fixing antique clocks in the living room, partly as a hobby and partly as a necessary source of income. Then within the space of three months both of her parents died. Soon after, she became depressed. She cried frequently and seemed anxious and restless. During the day, she found it difficult to remain seated for long, and during the night, she found it hard to sleep. She dreamed of her parents calling out to her and sometimes had nightmares of her children dying. She spoke of there being little purpose left for her in life.

Is this a picture of normal grief? Suppose she were to continue to feel like this for three months, or six months. Suppose, also, that she made deprecating remarks about herself, such as telling everyone that she was a bad mother and a bad wife. Do such preoccupations indicate that she needs treatment? Suppose, also, that she began to drink or to complain for no apparent reason that her husband was seeing another woman. Are such behaviors automatically pathological? Or can they exist in people who are emotionally well?

Similarly it may be difficult to decide whether a student who is anxious before an examination is excessively anxious, or whether a child frightened of the dark is unreasonably frightened; and whether, therefore, he merits concern. A proper answer comes out of knowing those particular persons and will depend on the details of that particular situation: on the importance to the student of the examination, or on the age of the child, or, perhaps, even on the degree of the darkness. Inevitably, in response to the ordinary stresses of life, people are troubled, sometimes to the point of distraction. To live at all is to be unhappy sometimes and irrational sometimes. Treatment becomes appropriate primarily when the person's emotional response is out of proportion to the circumstances of his life, for neither a psychiatrist nor anyone else can cancel out the ordinary pain of living. Distinguishing, therefore, between normal and abnormal behavior is no sterile academic exercise but is the first step in the therapeutic process.

Consider as a final example a twenty-three-year-old woman who came to therapy with the following symptoms: a loss of appetite, a sleep disturbance, and a pervasive feeling of sadness manifested by withdrawal from people and by episodes of crying—in short, the familiar symptoms of a depression. In addition she complained of a lifelong sense of inadequacy. She had always been frightened of new situations and new people. She felt that she was inhibited, even with her husband, a young law student whom she had married only a few months previously. Much of the time she found that she was uncomfortable with him or angry at him for no particular reason. Her irritation with him seemed to an extent to have affected their sexual life, for they were having intercourse perfunctorily and only once every three weeks.

The patient entered treatment, which continued over the next two years. Her depression lifted, as it frequently does, within the first few weeks. The focus of the remainder of treatment—insofar as the diffuse and roundabout process of psychotherapy can be said to have a focus—was on those experiences of her life that had to do with her feeling insecure and inhibited and that made her vulnerable to a depression in the first place. And therapy seemed to help: she became more self-confident and assertive, and she was happier. She opened a small shop and made a success of it. Her relationship with her husband also improved. They enjoyed each other's company and looked forward to being with each other. After two years of treatment she was asymptomatic—except for one thing. When she and her husband had sexual intercourse, it was still perfunctory and only about once every three weeks. Although the frequency of their sexual relations was much less than other couples their age, and apparently less satisfactory, neither one of them was concerned about it. They seemed content.

The therapist then had to decide whether he should use his great influence to draw the attention of his patient to this behavior, which was unusual if not abnormal, or whether he should leave well enough alone and allow treatment to come to an end. He asked two other psychiatrists for their opinion. The first commented that there must be some other underlying and fundamental discord between the couple, because there can be no true marriage in the absence of a sexual life. The other psychiatrist remarked blandly that he himself had intercourse once every three weeks. And so even experts cannot always agree on the limits of normal behavior. As it happened, the patient left treatment of her own accord a few weeks later.

If the manifestations of mental illness can only be seen in relief against normal behavior, what then, after all, is normal behavior? What sort of a person is a normal person? He is someone, first of all, who feels happy a considerable part of the time. Not all the time, of course. He is angry when he is frustrated, disappointed when he fails. He grieves when he has lost someone. Sometimes he is frightened. But he is not characteristically in any single mood, for there is an aptness to his feelings, a fit between them and the circumstances of his life. Since the circumstances of every person's life are varied, so are his feelings. Still, in general he thinks of himself as being happy. He can relate to other people, being assertive when appropriate and conciliatory at other times. He may not feel comfortable with everyone, but he does feel secure within his family and among his friends. And there are groups—religious, perhaps, or social—with whose members he feels an identity. And he can love, which means he can be trusting and affectionate. And he can make love without feeling oppressed or uncomfortable. Such a person often finds himself committed to other people, or even to an idea, to a degree where he loses himself in a larger purpose. Consequently when he has children, he becomes part of them and continues on in their lives, so that personal death becomes less real and less frightening. A normal person can work with satisfaction, if it is decent work; and he can relax when he is not working. He enjoys play. In fact he enjoys himself much of the time, even if he is only talking to a friend or watching television. But probably the defining quality of a normal person is a kind of flexibility that allows him to adapt to the different demands and stresses that life imposes upon him. He can tolerate conflict and frustration and loneliness—to some extent. And he is able to seize upon life, too. He is successful at work and with people and within his family—to some extent.

Probably it is possible to go on endlessly sketching the form of an ideal human being, but as he is drawn more and more precisely, he less and less resembles anyone in the real world. And yet there are normal people.

Perhaps it is easier to say what is not meant by normal than what is. Normal is not average. If someone could be average in every conceivable way, he could still be disturbed, although a perfectly average man is no more real than someone who is perfectly normal. Conversely, being atypical does not mean someone is sick. A man may still be normal who every day sleeps only five hours, works an extra full-time job, and takes three showers. But knowing just how someone deviates from the average is important in understanding him, for three reasons:

1. Although a particular behavior may not be in itself abnormal, it may be part of a pattern that reflects an abnormal process. Sleeping less than average, for instance, is sometimes associated with severe depressions and other psychoses. Also, if someone is extremely far from average in some respect of behavior or attitude, it is likely he will turn out to be emotionally ill by some other criteria.

2. Someone who is significantly different from other people may be under special strain as a result, for in order to be with people, it is necessary to do pretty much the things other people do. A man who works two full-time jobs, for instance, is not likely to be at home when his family is. If he is away from the important people in his life most of the time, to some extent, inevitably, he will be emotionally deprived.

3. But most important, an individual is most himself at just those points where he is different from others. Consequently these are points of departure for a search into an understanding of him. Human behavior is always hard to understand, for it is an expression for the most part of unconscious wishes and conflicts; nevertheless, personality becomes tangible in these out-of-the-ordinary habits and attitudes. One may ask why, for instance, a man would take three showers every day. It may be because he thinks of himself or his body as being unclean; or he might find a sensual pleasure in rubbing himself; or there might be countless other reasons, any of which may illuminate a facet of his personality. Knowing what is special about someone is knowing, at least, what is worth paying attention to and what to ask about.

Normal also does not mean *adjusted*, if that word is used to refer to someone who accepts the dominant ethic of a particular society. For one thing, that ethic is frequently not what it pretends to be. The unwritten rules that govern sexual behavior in this country, for example, are scarcely those that issue from the pulpit. Even such a fundament of civilization as the law, which is spoken of invariably with esteem, is treated actually with bland disregard. People are not really expected to obey the law a substantial amount of the time, any more than they are expected to work a full day or to keep every promise they make. But even were society more consistent, there would still be room for an unconventional person. At every extreme of social custom there are normal people, and creative, valuable people.

Normal does not refer to a state of being at all, but rather to a process, the process of growing up and into life. Adolescence has been described as a continual adjustment to the business of growing up, but that adjustment goes on at every age. Somewhere along the way, if a person is healthy, he learns to be himself and to fulfill himself, but the process is never complete. He may know himself, but never altogether, for he is always changing. If he is unable to change enough to compensate for new circumstances in his life, then he will develop an emotional disorder. For that reason emotional illnesses may always be regarded as failures of adaptation.

So if mental health is a process of growth, mental illness is an inhibition of that process. If being normal is to work and love and feel happy—relatively—being disturbed emotionally is to suffer relative impairment in these capacities. There is not yet a better distinction between health and illness or between an ordinary person and a patient. In practice a therapist draws on the sum of his training and his experience as a human being to look àt another human being and the sum of *his* experience, and then, in that context, come to a judgment about whether that other person needs help and whether he can provide it. In this final analysis it is an intuitive rather than a systematic judgment—but adequate for the most part.

It would be easier to decide if someone were sick if the underlying causes of mental illness were less obscure. Long ago it was thought that lunacy was related to the phases of the moon, or to an imbalance of humours or fluids within the body, or to an improper diet. There has been real and unmistakable progress since that time, but if one were to pick up a current psychiatric journal, he would still see, although couched in somewhat different language, more or less the same sort of explanations given for more or less the same conditions. Nowadays, for bodily humours, read biogenic amines, and for improper diet, substitute vitamin deficiencies. As for the phases of the moon, researchers are still correlating outbreaks of emotional illness with the full moon. In addition we are led to believe by different psychiatrists that mental illnesses are caused by rhythmic, electrical discharges in the brain; disturbances of breast-feeding; insufficient lithium salts in the drinking water; an allergic reaction; a society that tolerates poverty and pollution; an excess of hormones—or a deficiency; or the *Föhn*, which is a hot wind that blows up into Europe from the Mediterranean. Even so, the fact is, the study of mental illness is slowly coming to rest on a body of knowledge rather than opinion. That knowledge is drawn not only from psychology, but from all the biological and behavioral sciences. The important current theories of mental illness that have emerged tend to fall into two significant types, which should be understood because they reflect contrasting views of human nature.

One primary class of theories attributes mental illness to psychological causes. The best example is psychoanalysis, including its various offshoots, the Jungian and Adlerian schools and the neo-Freudian schools. A second example, with somewhat different origins and emphases, is existential psychoanalysis. There are subschools within these schools. Each of these theories or philosophies is distinguished carefully from the others by its parochial advocates in a great volume of professional literature that seems to concern itself in large part with exploring its own terminology. Nevertheless, in their conception of the individual, they resemble each other closely. These theories see man as being, throughout his life, in dynamic balance, in terms of his changing inner self, his needs and conflicts, and his changing relationships with others. They conceive him in terms of those qualities of mind or spirit that he reports of himself and that we all recognize in ourselves, namely our feelings, thoughts, desires, ambitions, and memories. These facets of man, and also his emotional disturbances, are viewed as an outgrowth of his past, of his particular history and especially his childhood. Also, increasingly, these theories recognize man as one individual among a family or a community. If he is disturbed, his illness is manifest in the dynamics within these social groups; in turn, disturbances of these groups are manifest within him, for he is one strand of a web made up of people. He learns about the world through the lines of communication along this web; if those lines are tangled, he is likely to misunderstand the world. Mental illness is regarded as a distortion of some aspect of growing up that leaves behind such a misunderstanding. On the basis of that misconception the disturbed individual mishandles the world. He searches for the wrong things in the wrong places. He protects himself in the wrong ways. He asks the wrong questions and gets the wrong answers, so he never learns. Since he does not know how to live, his needs go unfulfilled, and he is unhappy.

A somewhat contrasting theory of psychology comes from the work of Pavlov and others on learning in animals. His discoveries have been found to apply to people as well and are beginning to have a considerable influence on American psychiatry. The emphasis of the theory is on the observable behavior of man rather than on his inner life, what he does rather than what he feels. Neurotic behavior is viewed as an error in learning which has occurred in the past and has persisted into the present as a bad habit. The adherents of this theory, the behaviorists, are more likely than psychoanalysts to experiment and to measure the results of treatment. They are also more likely to concentrate on symptoms rather than causes. Still, they too think of psychological symptoms as being psychologically caused. Emotional illness, in their judgment, grows out of conflict and anxiety, very much as the psychoanalysts believe. In short, like the psychoanalysts, they view each person as an individual who is the sum of his past, and who is struggling on that basis to cope with a changing and unpredictable present.

But there is another view of man, which sees him not so much as a person whom we can understand intuitively because we are like him, but rather as a machine, with an exceedingly complicated mechanism vulnerable to the smallest defect of its parts and sensitive to the smallest change in the manner of its operation. It is a piece-by-piece analysis which considers the human being in terms of his nervous system and endocrine system, for instance, and then in terms of the organs that participate in those systems—the limbic lobe of the brain, for example, or the adrenal cortex—and focuses, then, ever more precisely onto still smaller and more delicate structures, until the single nerve cell comes into view and the still smaller bits of chemicals and enzymes which are secreted by the nerve endings, these last exceedingly tiny substances controlled in part by genes and controlling in turn all of behavior and all of life. No one likes to represent his ideas in just such terms, for it is an unattractive thesis for man, who has not yet become accustomed to thinking of himself as only one animal among others, without having to consider that he is even less, only a machine, or a thing. But, of course, man is a thing like anything else in the world and governed by the same physical laws that describe a tree or a rock. He too is only the sum of his parts. Those theories that contemplate man from this microscopic perspective speak in the vernacular of chemistry and neurophysiology and other obscure disciplines that are not understood by most psychiatrists, who are inclined as a group to be more philosophical than scientific. But they understand well enough the importance of the tools that have been delivered to them through research in these fields. Advances in psychopharmacology alone have changed the entire practice of psychiatry over the last twenty-five years, particularly the management of the serious mental illnesses that are the subject of this book. Nevertheless these theories do not offer an overall account of human behavior. They cannot explain why someone quarrels with his in-laws or wears his tie askew or believes in God; but they are able to explain isolated fragments of behavior, such as the outbursts of temper associated with electrical discharges in the temporal lobe of the brain. Similarly they have shown that the mental changes of general paresis are due to syphilis, and that vascular disease in certain areas of the brain prevent the conceptualization of speech, and that some forms of mental retardation are caused by enzymatic deficiencies and prevented by special diet, and that thyroid dysfunction can cause depression or anxiety or frank psychosis—and so on.

Every mental illness or disturbance of behavior can be viewed, therefore, either as *organic* in origin—the result of a bodily defect of some sort; or *functional*—the result of a psychological conflict or trauma. There are some who explain all of mental illness, despite its extraordinary diversity, exclusively from one point of view or the other. On one side there are those who say that the symptoms of emotional illness in a particular person are no more or less than the signs of a disordered nervous system, and so can be understood without recourse to examining that person's life. They may go on to point out that many qualities of the personality, intelligence, liveliness, and sensitivity are shaped by the time of birth, and that even complicated patterns of living that occur much later on, such as criminality or senility, are predetermined genetically. If it were so, it would be as if a man's destiny were fixed forever in his genes, and life itself only a redundant postscript to the moment of conception. At the other pole there are those who attribute every experience of an individual, whether it is illness, financial failure, or a bad marriage, to the unconscious needs of that individual to have that experience. By this conceit, there is no reality at all outside of the mind. There are no independent, accidental events, no luck. Whatever ill befalls man, he is to blame for it, or his upbringing. If he does not grow, it is because unconsciously he does not wish to grow. If he does not thrive, it is because he does not wish to thrive. Diabetes and cancer and all physical diseases are psychosomatic. Growing old and dying are not required, but are only the waning of the will to live.

Naturally most psychologists and psychiatrists do not subscribe to such extreme positions. Concerned as they are with the real problems of real people, they cannot allow themselves to squeeze their clinical judgment into an ideology; but since they need to know the causes of mental illness in order to diagnose and especially in order to treat, they must concern themselves in every condition they study with these two contrasting conceptions of man. All the important psychiatric conditions have still these two parallel explanations. Schizophrenia, for example, is being actively investigated now by chemists who think they have found in the urine of patients substances that are chemically similar in structure to the common hallucinogens such as mescaline. It is thought that this disease represents an inborn, probably hereditary, error of metabolism in which ordinary neurotransmitters are transformed into psychomimetic compounds which provoke hallucinations and other symptoms of psychosis. At the same time, serious work by family therapists has suggested that the pathogenesis of schizophrenia is related to distinctive and abnormal relationships within the families of schizophrenics. The relationship between a schizophrenic and his mother is especially strained and clouded. His illness is considered to be in part an attempt to escape from the conflicts that that relationship imposes upon him. There are thousands of other ongoing studies of schizophrenia, but they all proceed down these two major avenues of inquiry: into the psychological and organic causes of the disease. Similarly there are, still, opposing theories that relate homosexuality to abnormal levels of hormones in the blood, or, on the other hand, to improper rearing during the first two years of life. Depression is still explained in psychological terms as an inability to express anger effectively, and, at the same time, as a deficiency of noradrenaline in the infinitesimal spaces between the nerve endings of the brain. Alcoholism is attributed by some to a specific genetic vulnerability, and by others to a specific type of personality. And so on. Occasionally an illness thought by some to be psychogenic turns out because of some obvious reason to be unequivocally physical in origin; but for most psychiatric conditions, there is not sufficient evidence to declare one formulation right and the other wrong. The orientation of a given psychiatrist may depend only on whether he feels more comfortable talking to a patient or giving him an injection.

This philosophical dichotomy, which seems to be inescapable, has a long and troublesome history, for it is an outgrowth of our basic difficulty in thinking about ourselves objectively, in distinguishing our minds, with which we are familiar, from our brains, which we know only by reputation, as scientists tell us about them. The two are not identical. The fact is, a mental disturbance is not equivalent exactly to a malfunction of the brain. Sometimes, therefore, in order to understand someone, particularly if he is emotionally disturbed, it becomes necessary to understand him both from a psychological and from a physiological point of view—in terms of his mind, and also in terms of his body and brain.

A twenty-year-old man was brought to the admitting office of a psychiatric hospital, screaming that a banshee was after him. He was otherwise incoherent. He mumbled and his speech was slurred. No information could be obtained from him, for he would not reply to questions. He did not seem to know where he was. He talked to himself and sometimes shied away suddenly as if there were something invisible in the room, threatening him. When he was not cringing behind a desk, he paced restlessly. His appearance was unkempt, as if he had slept in his clothes or not slept at all. He was sweating profusely and there was a gross tremor of his hands. Also his temperature was somewhat elevated.

His fever dropped within a few hours, but otherwise his condition remained remarkably the same for the next three weeks. He was agitated, hallucinating, and delusional. His thinking was disorganized, and he remained frightened and, at times, terror-stricken. He was, in short, grossly psychotic. After a while, however, he came to know that he was in a hospital, and he was able to reply somewhat to questions. The significant elements of his history, as it was obtained from him, his friends, and his mother, were as follows:

He was the first child born to a middle-aged couple of Irish extraction. His father was a gruff but likable man who had become successful in a small business. His mother was an attractive woman who was said to have had great charm. She always dressed and appeared much younger than her true age. The patient's birth was followed three years later by the birth of a younger brother, who was, unfortunately, mongoloid. The focus of the patient's early life was this defective brother, for the child took up much of his parents' attention. When the patient was ten, he himself was given a principal responsibility for caring for his brother. At about the same time, his parents began to show evidence of some emotional difficulty. His father, who had always drunk to a degree, now became frankly alcoholic. His mother became intermittently depressed. Her youthfulness seemed now to be childishness. She leaned heavily on the patient despite his very young age.

She kissed him for his every good deed and reminded him continually of how she relied on him to be the man of the family. Sometimes these intimate scenes were uncomfortable to people who witnessed them. But when she became very depressed, she rejected her son. She accused him of driving her into a mental hospital, where her brother, who was schizophrenic, had been for years. At these times of particular upset, she used tranquilizers in high doses.

The first sign of any emotional illness in the patient occurred when he was twelve. The level of his work in school dropped. He stayed home from school frequently with stomachaches or was truant with friends. And he began experiencing recurrent nightmares in which his brother was killed. Nevertheless, after a while, he began to do well again. He was asymptomatic until the age of seventeen, when his father died in an automobile accident. Abruptly he dropped out of school. He spent his days by himself, either in his room or walking in the vicinity of his home. Also he developed a short-lived fear of riding in automobiles. In those first days of his bereavement he seemed to his mother to be numb more than depressed. After some months he became more communicative with his friends, but his relationship with her became more distant. He stayed away from home for increasingly long periods, and he began to drink. He worked intermittently at his father's business and stayed at those times with his mother and brother; the rest of the time he stayed with friends. Twice, along with his friends, he was arrested on drug charges but released each time on condition he go into psychotherapy. Both treatments ended after only a few visits when he refused to continue. His abuse of drugs had by then included amphetamines, cocaine, and barbiturates, none of them very frequently. But he used marijuana and LSD many times, and, of course, alcohol.

A few days prior to his admission the patient, who had never gone out with girls, was maneuvered as a joke by his friends into dating a prostitute. What happened was not known, but he seemed to take the joke in bad grace. He was angry and upset. Since then he had had little to drink or eat until a few hours prior to his admission when, as he had done frequently before, he ingested a tablet of LSD. This time, however, he promptly developed the florid psychosis described above.

This meager information, this small summary of a life, was all the psychiatrist had to enable him to understand his patient. Neither were all the significant events of that life underlined as they would be, perhaps, in a novel. There were only diffuse and random happenings telling no special story, or perhaps telling many stories. The task of the therapist always is to decide which happenings have meaning to his patient, or, in other words, which of the stories of his life is the story of his illness. To that end, he draws up in his mind a theoretical scheme that, if he is adroit or sensitive, explains his patient more or less. This formulation is not framed exclusively in psychological terms or in biological terms but in bits of one and fragments of the other, for reasons that are apparent, for example, in the investigation of this particular patient by the particular psychiatrist charged with the responsibility for his care.

When the patient arrived at the admitting office, it was obvious, almost at first glance, that he was psychotic. The term *psychosis* is defined usually as a serious disorganization of personality which causes the individual to be unable to distinguish reality; but since no one in the world distinguishes reality exactly, the word has come to be used within the profession only to refer to a very severe degree of illness. Certain symptoms, such as hallucinations or delusions, always imply psychosis, by consensus. And certain diseases, such as schizophrenia or manic-depressive illness, once diagnosed in a patient, are thought always to be lurking beneath the surface, so that such a patient, even when otherwise entirely well, is said to have an underlying psychosis. Used in this sense, the term loses even its general descriptive value. In addition, anyone sufficiently peculiar may be described as "bizarre" and said to be psychotic. This patient then was plainly psychotic, but the etiology of his psychosis was not plain. Schizophrenia, which is the most common psychosis in this age group, does not usually present with visual hallucinations, slurring of speech, or a fever. And unless the schizophrenic is so preoccupied with his thoughts, so autistic, that he is entirely out of contact with his surroundings, he is not usually disoriented, despite his psychosis. He knows where he is and who he is and what day and what month it is. Such symptoms are more typical of organic psychoses. In this context *organic* refers to a great host of physical disorders of the brain or of any of the more important organs of the body. They include vascular, metabolic, infectious, and neoplastic diseases, and others. They include, also, drug-induced psychoses, which, unfortunately, are also common at this age. Another familiar organic psychosis is delirium tremens, abbreviated usually to DTs, and it is the most important of the various abnormal states of mind related to alcoholism. Like any medical condition, delirium tremens can be present with only one or another of its principal manifestations, but most commonly it manifests itself as a syndrome that is a collection of associated symptoms. Characteristically, a man who has used alcohol to excess for many years stops drinking abruptly and within one or two days begins to shake and experience visual or tactile hallucinations, usually frightening. He may run a fever. He may also convulse or die; otherwise, with proper treatment, the condition usually resolves within a few days.

As an initial task, then, the psychiatrist had to judge if this young man's psychosis was an atypical presentation of schizophrenia or whether it was due to the ingestion of LSD, or whether it had some other cause. In particular he had to rule out delirium tremens, since that illness is a potentially life-

threatening illness. Some elements of the history were sugges-
tive of delirium tremens, as was the presence of a fever. But
the patient's temperature was not so high that it was not consistent also with the simple dehydration that results from not
drinking any fluids for a few days. Primarily because of the
young age of the patient, the psychiatrist concluded tentatively that his psychosis was probably attributable more to the
effect of the hallucinogen than to delirium tremens, although,
of course, an illness may have more than one contributing
cause. In this young man the complication of his sudden
withdrawal from alcohol may have explained why he suffered
such a devastating reaction to LSD on this occasion and never
previously. On the other hand the specific effect of LSD is
determined in part by the user's state of mind. His terrified
condition may have reflected only the anxiety and depression
he was already feeling at the time he took the drug.

Treatment was begun at once in the admitting office. An attempt was made to calm the patient by assuring him that he
was safe. He was encouraged to sit quietly and also to drink
and eat. He was brought then to a psychiatric ward, where he
was kept under close supervision in a well-lit, quiet room.
Also he was given small amounts of phenothiazines, which is a
major class of tranquilizing drugs. Over the next few days this
medication was given to him in increasingly large doses with
only the poor results described above.

At this point the patient's illness had lasted too long to be
consistent with the diagnosis of delirium tremens. After three
further weeks of little improvement the clinical course was
unusually long even for an LSD psychosis. The psychiatrist
then was forced to consider that the patient may have been
schizophrenic after all, although the schizophrenic reaction
could easily have been precipitated by the LSD, or by the
abuse of alcohol, or for that matter, by the emotional stress of
his encounter with the prostitute, coming as it did in the context of the larger stress of the death of his father. In further

support of the diagnosis of schizophrenia was the uncle's illness, for schizophrenia tends to be familial.

The process, then, by which a psychiatrist diagnoses a psychosis is the same as that employed by any physician to diagnose any physical ailment: he matches up the signs and symptoms that appear in his patient against a set of distinctive clinical syndromes. Even when these syndromes are defined partly by characteristic laboratory findings—as psychiatric conditions are not usually—they are still only Platonic ideals which are never realized fully in any particular patient. And so no patient is really a classic case of any illness, but only an approximation. Yet diagnosis is important, for usually it determines treatment.

Once the clinician steps away from the psychoses to the less extreme emotional disorders, such as the neuroses or the disorders of personality and character, he speaks in terms of syndromes that are still less clearly defined and still less fully exemplified by any particular patient. These are conditions defined not by etiology but by one or two of their most prominent symptoms—such as the obsessive-compulsive neurosis, the depressive neurosis, the withdrawal reaction of childhood, or one or another of the sexual disturbances. And most typically they are explained not in the biological terms that seem more and more appropriate to the understanding of the psychoses, even the so-called functional psychoses, but in psychological terms.

This young man who was so terribly ill, so suddenly, did not arrive at his illness overnight. The twenty years he had lived previously were relevant to the shape and substance of his psychosis as it finally came upon him. The psychiatrist, therefore, could not comfort himself with the thought that he truly understood his patient when at last he had determined that the man was schizophrenic, assuming he really knew even that much. Even with only a summary of his patient's life to guide him, he had to go further and construe what little he knew into a coherent picture that placed in perspective the important elements of that life's experience. There is a logic to every person's existence that lends it a special continuity and character. The clinician tries to compose what he can see of that logic into a psychodynamic formulation. This is an account of the important experiences of a person's past life and his reactions to those experiences. It describes his emotional conflicts and the devices he uses for coping with them. In short it is a description of his personality. Such a formulation takes the shape of a set of theoretical references. For example, a formulation describing this young schizophrenic man would have tried to make sense out of his current illness in terms of his past life. It would have explored some of the following issues:

He was born to parents already past the usual childbearing age. That circumstance alone raises a number of questions: why was it that they had had no children previously? Did they intend not to? And did they intend for the patient to be born, or was he an unwanted child? Even twenty years later it would have been important to establish that fact, were it possible, for the wish of a couple to have a particular child is an indicator of the emotional climate in which he will live subsequently. At any rate his arrival, sought or unsought, must at least have implied a disruption in the accustomed habits of his parents. Even with younger parents, less set in their ways, the birth of a first child marks a division in life more significant than any other single event. But exactly how this particular family lived for the next three years was not known.

The first signal event in the patient's life was, as it sometimes is, the birth of a younger sibling. If it is ordinary for a child to have feelings of rivalry and resentment for an ordinary sibling who competes for the attention of his parents, how much worse those feelings must be when that sibling requires more than the usual care and attention. Anger is felt blindly by children as a wish to injure or annihilate. The patient must have felt that strongly, and because his brother was indeed damaged, he must also have felt guilty, for wishes are experienced by children as being real and as making real things happen. Perhaps if he had had parents who understood, they could have protected him against these impulses and reassured him. Instead, because of their own weaknesses, they thrust him more forcibly into this arena of conflict by demanding that he be responsible for his brother. Consequently he felt still more resentment. The recurrent nightmares of his brother's death were a disguised wish to be rid of him. That they were cast in the form of nightmares is an indication of the anxiety and guilt he must also have felt.

And if he had to be a parent to his brother, who was there to be a parent to him? His father was alcoholic and his mother was not infrequently depressed. She was also immature, and seductive to him in a manner just short of being overtly sexual. Of course, as everyone knows nowadays, it is a common if not universal fantasy for a child to wish to possess the parent of the opposite sex, sexually and otherwise. At the same time, in his mind he does away with the parent of the same sex. Like any other fantasy, it makes no problem unless it threatens to become real, but in the life of this child it was threatening to become real. So he had to feel guilty also about displacing his father. With the egotism of a child he would have blamed himself then for his father's retreat into alcohol. Obviously he was not satisfying his mother's needs either, whatever they were, so he had that to blame himself for too.

There was no apparent reason for the patient developing symptoms at the age of twelve rather than at ten or even at a younger age. Perhaps the seductive behavior of his mother became more threatening to him when he entered puberty, or perhaps there was an entirely different stress coming from school or from his relationships with his peers. He must have been upset at school, for he avoided it and began to do poorly academically. And stomachaches such as those that caused him to stay at home are commonly associated with school problems. They are an example, the only example in his case, of a psychophysiologic reaction, which is a dysfunction of certain organ systems as the result of emotional stress or conflict. Such symptoms are a major route of the expression of unconscious conflict.

These relatively minor and relatively common symptoms were a background to the severe disturbance the patient developed after his father died. The fact of death is always frightening, and frightening especially to someone who fantasizes or dreams about death, for it makes the fantasy seem more real. Such a fantasy probably underlay his fear of riding in automobiles. It was a symbolic expression of a fear of losing control of himself in a context where losing control might have meant killing himself or killing someone else, as his father was killed in a car. But this phobic symptom was only one portion of a distress greatly beyond that of an ordinary bereavement. His father's death precipitated within him an emotional upheaval latent in his personality as a result of his previous experiences. If he had previously somewhat displaced his father at home, he had now displaced him altogether; with no one to stand between him and his seductive mother, he drew away from her into himself. He left school and he left home. Finally, in a more striking withdrawal, he resorted to a device that he had learned about from his parents, the use of alcohol and drugs.

Alcohol serves a number of purposes simultaneously. It is a tranquilizer of sorts and it relieves or at least obscures the symptoms of depression. For someone who is inhibited and afraid of people, it is a clouded lens through which the world looks less forbidding. And for someone who feels guilty, it is its own punishment. More important for this young man, becoming an alcoholic was to become like his father, which was a way of retaining him and clinging to him even after he had died.

The fact that the patient at the age of twenty had not yet gone out with women suggests a sexual conflict, which was probably an outgrowth of his relationship with his mother. Every mother is the prototype of all women to her children; if she is extraordinarily threatening, all women become threatening. Even under favorable circumstances, the ability to behave sexually, like most complicated human activity, is learned a little bit at a time. If someone is frightened of sex, he learns even more slowly. If someone is very frightened, as this man was, it is not helpful to him to arrange an assignation with a prostitute, any more than it would help someone afraid of the water to be thrown into the deep end of a pool. Perhaps it was this final injury that provoked his psychotic break.

The foregoing is not an inclusive or exhaustive explanation of a human being. It is a system of suppositions that are only the bare bones of an explanation and that are tentative and speculative until they are fleshed out by the patient's own memories offered in his own words—and by his further experiences. Indeed, because they are only suppositions, they may turn out to be wrong, however reasonable they seem at first; and if they seem unreasonable at first, even absurd, they may nevertheless turn out to be right. There was much more to know about this patient than could be guessed at initially. Even after years of analytic inquiry, there would be more to know.

At the time of the patient's psychosis there were additional questions of interest to the psychiatrist. Assuming his patient hallucinated because of the effect of LSD or because he was schizophrenic, why did he hallucinate a banshee? According to Irish mythology, the banshee is a harbinger of death; was he then still preoccupied with his father's death? Or was it someone else's death he was imagining? Perhaps this single symptom illustrates by itself the point of the entire case history, which is that the behavior of people cannot be described adequately from any single, fixed theoretical point of view, either biological or psychological, but only by both in the context of each other, and even then only in tantalizing approximation.

2 THE TREATMENT OF MENTAL ILLNESS

SINCE mental illness is so complex, it might be argued that its treatment should rest exclusively in the hands of professionals. Certainly on occasion it must. The management of an acutely psychotic person requires not only the close attention of a psychiatrist, but also that of a number of people highly trained in other disciplines: psychologists, social workers, nurses, and often neurologists and other physicians. The more acute the illness, the closer this supervision needs to be. But there are other times, in fact most of the time, when the care of the mentally ill is dispensed necessarily by those who are largely untrained, this group including, for example, ministers, welfare workers, school counselors, parole officers, and a great many others, and including especially members of the affected person's family. Their help is not simply a minor portion of what a psychiatrist or psychologist might offer if they could be around more constantly, but rather something special, which goes beyond what anyone else can do. This is so in part precisely because such an illness is complex. Although most serious emotional disorders intermittently become acute, they manifest themselves over long periods of time in many ways, and consequently must be attacked in a variety of ways by all those with whom the sick person has a relationship. In the long run it is they who most profoundly influence the course of that person's illness.

Consider again the young man described at the end of the last chapter. We may call him John.

John spent exactly one month in the hospital. At the time of his discharge he was considerably improved, although not entirely well. He no longer hallucinated and was able to think clearly, but he seemed withdrawn and somewhat depressed. He continued taking medication in somewhat decreased doses and began visiting a psychiatrist once a week. This program of treatment—intermittent use of medication in varying doses and weekly visits to a psychiatrist—continued over the next five years, during which time he was not hospitalized again. At the end of that period he was employed successfully, attending night school, and married. If he was schizophrenic still, he showed no overt evidence of it. By the usual standards by which a young man's adjustment might be measured, he was doing well. It could scarcely be said, though, that those five years went smoothly. There were long periods when he continued drinking to excess and using drugs. There were other times when he became so suspicious of the people around him that he could reasonably be described as paranoid. But besides these obvious signs of psychopathology, he was disturbed in more pedestrian ways. He had trouble making friends. He had trouble dating, and he had sexual difficulties. He had trouble remaining in class without becoming panicky. His stomach complaints returned from time to time, and he had other physical symptoms. Because he tended to think people were unfair to him, he had trouble holding onto a job.

Over the course of those five years he met a number of people who influenced him one way or the other; but besides his psychiatrist there were four people without whose help he could not have done as well as he did.

The first was his sponsor at Alcoholics Anonymous. A year subsequent to his discharge from the hospital John was once again drinking very heavily. One weekend he was arrested, charged with driving his car while intoxicated. The judge placed him on probation on condition that he join Alcoholics Anonymous. Over the next few months he made friends with, then asked to have as a sponsor, a middle-aged man with whom from then on he maintained a stormy but very close relationship. At various times, sometimes in the middle of the night, this older man came to John's apartment to dissuade him when he was on the verge of drinking or to take away the bottle if he had already started. He was always available by telephone if John was feeling anxious or agitated. He was supportive. Often he invited John to his home for dinner and to a considerable degree made him feel like a member of the family, even to the extent of fighting with him. He encouraged him to get a job and when he lost it to get another. He helped him fill out an application for night school, and then delivered the application personally. When John was having problems dating, he was there to commiserate with him and tell him about all the problems he had had when he was that age. In such ways he was steadfastly helpful and encouraging.

An English teacher, recognizing John's difficulty speaking in class, drew him aside and suggested he transfer to a smaller class where he could be supervised more closely and come to know the other students better. John agreed to the transfer, but returned frequently to visit with this particular teacher and ultimately become friends with him. He came for advice mostly, not only on such academic matters as how to take proper notes or how to study for an examination, but also how to change a flat tire, how to clean a furnace, how to cook steaks, and more important, how to deal with people: how to respond to a scolding from a boss, how to behave on a double date, how to make conversation at a party, and so on. If John felt he was being persecuted, his teacher helped him to determine what was really happening. He helped him, in short, to understand what other people were feeling and how to react to them.

Because John was preoccupied with physical symptoms, he spent considerable time visiting his family doctor, a sympathetic and patient woman. Sometimes his worries about his health reached delusional proportions. He thought he might have cancer. She examined him carefully each time, then informed him that he was not suffering from any such serious disease. At other times, over and over again, she had to convince him that he was not developing some obscure heart ailment just because he had palpitations when he was anxious. When he tried to have sexual intercourse again, he discovered himself to be impotent, and she had to assure him then that he was not sexually disabled by some physical disease. By being calm herself, she was able to calm him. By being optimistic, she helped him to think he might overcome his sexual conflicts, and in time he did. At the age of twenty-four he married.

His wife became the most important person in his life. No short paragraph could describe the extent of her influence. She was in every part of his life. She worked with him, worried with him, made plans with him. She listened to him when he was upset. She made friends for the two of them. She helped him with his schoolwork, typing up his papers. She acted as referee when he and his mother were quarreling. When he left a job impulsively, she convinced him to return to it. When he had plainly undertaken too much, she described his failure as temporary and unimportant, and she encouraged him to try again. Since she lived with him, she knew before anyone else when he was becoming depressed or paranoid. Consequently she was an important source of information for his psychiatrist. Sometimes, on the psychiatrist's instructions, she would regulate his medication. She took on this responsibility without undermining his self-respect. She was accepting of his weaknesses, but she believed in him. Perhaps in these matters she was doing only those things that a wife might be expected to do; but to someone unsure of himself, as John was, she meant the difference between failure and success, or the difference between being sick and being well.

These various people whose relationships to John made such a difference in his life were providing, whether they realized it or not, supportive psychotherapy. Whether they went by the name of friend or family or physician, they were acting much of the time as therapist. As is plain from these examples, such collateral therapists act in a way complementary to that of the psychiatrist or psychologist. Sometimes their roles are overlapping, sometimes distinct. To better define each of these roles, it is helpful to know how a psychiatrist or psychologist goes about evaluating a patient and what sort of treatment alternatives are open to him. Depending on the nature of treatment and the place of treatment, the collateral therapist has a different set of tasks to perform.

THE ROLE OF THE PROFESSIONAL

Evaluation

The treatment of the emotionally disturbed person is founded, of course, on a proper understanding of him, not only as a person with particular problems, but as a particular human being. But coming to know him is not easy. Even when he comes willingly for help, he may hesitate to talk about the intimate details of his life. He may think of himself as abused or mistreated, and consequently be mistrustful. He may think of himself as a failure, and be ashamed. And he may be unwilling to admit to another person—or to himself—how upset, or how ill, he really is. And certain conditions may exhaust him emotionally so that he is unable to communicate his feelings at all. Sometimes he may not know himself well enough to explain himself to someone else.

In order to evaluate such a person successfully, and certainly in order to form a therapeutic relationship with him, the therapist must take into consideration that person's anxieties and uncertainties. He must show proper concern for his feelings. He shouldn't rush to give advice, but he should indicate even during the first interview some reason to be hopeful. Throughout their relationship, but especially during those first few encounters, he must be respectful, courteous, and friendly. He should be straightforward, able to discuss personal matters without embarrassment. He should be tactful, able to inquire about the patient's distress without upsetting him further. Finally, he should be patient. Although he wants, and perhaps needs, to know everything at once, he will learn about his patient only a little bit at a time. Obviously, interviewing someone properly requires skill.

The Initial Interviews

The information that is obtained about a patient during the first few interviews is usually organized to conform to the following outline:

THE CHIEF COMPLAINT: the patient's account, or the account of his family, of those difficulties that have led him to seek treatment.

THE PRESENT ILLNESS: an account of the way those difficulties have developed, usually over the last few days or weeks. Of course, emotional illnesses do not usually begin abruptly. They grow imperceptibly out of previous patterns of behavior, and so this account includes all previous symptoms and previous episodes of emotional distress.

PAST HISTORY: a summary of those aspects of the patient's life that tend to have emotional significance and that, when taken together, serve to define him as an individual. Included are the events of childhood. The patient's earliest memories are especially important because they describe experiences of special emotional impact, and because they illuminate his current state of mind. For example, people who are depressed tend to remember unhappy experiences.

A detailed history is taken also in these areas of the patient's life:

1. Physical and emotional development—including emotional disturbances of childhood, such as bed-wetting and night terrors.

2. School performance—including relationships with teachers and peers.

3. Work performance—including the details of any impairment of functioning.

4. Menstrual and sexual behavior—including attitudes toward all sexual experiences and including, in a woman, the emotional reaction to menarche.

5. Social history—including the range and depth of friendships.

6. Marital history—including all those petty circumstances that illuminate a relationship between husband and wife.

And, as they seem important, the patient's physical health, religious practices, financial condition, hobbies, and so on. These facts should coalesce into a picture of his personality, which makes clear his attitudes, interests, moral standards, ambitions—in short, the sum of himself.

FAMILY HISTORY: The largest influence on a person's life is unmistakably his family. It is important to know, therefore, as much as possible about the patient's parents and his siblings, especially as they seemed to him when he was growing up. Specific memories are more helpful than global characterizations, since everyone tends to idealize or caricature his parents. Enough should be known about all of the important people in the patient's life, including his children, so that they come alive in the therapist's mind as particular human beings.

Such a biography describes the patient in terms of his past and the course his illness has taken so far. Another perspective is obtained by describing him as he appears at present during the course of an interview. That examination is recorded in the form of a mental status.

The Mental Status

APPEARANCE AND BEHAVIOR—including, for example, patterns of dress and personal grooming, level of physical activity such as restlessness or agitation, bodily and facial expressions, and any peculiarities of appearance such as tics or spasms. Also the patient's reaction to the interviewer is observed.

CHARACTERISTICS OF SPEECH AND LANGUAGE—particularly as they reflect the formal qualities of thinking. Of special importance is the continuity of thought.

EMOTIONAL STATE—including not only prominent and pervasive moods such as depression or anxiety, but also those subtle shifts of feeling that characterize the interaction between any two people engaged in a conversation. The appropriateness and the range of emotional reactivity are noted. Anyone who is depressed is asked plainly if he is so upset that he is thinking of killing himself, and an estimation of the risk of suicide is made.

CONTENT OF THOUGHT—including special preoccupations such as obsessions, delusions, bodily concerns, and so on. Hallucinations and other disturbances of perception are noted.

INTELLECTUAL FUNCTIONING—including the ability to remember, to concentrate, to calculate arithmetically, and to think abstractedly. The patient is tested to see how well he is oriented to time and to his circumstances. And some determination is made about the patient's judgment and his insight into the nature of his illness.

Based on the patient's clinical history and mental status, the person evaluating him—who is likely to be a psychiatrist if the patient is suffering acutely from any of the serious illnesses described in this book—makes the following determinations:

DIAGNOSIS: Not simply a label by which to refer to the patient, but a dynamic formulation which takes into account the psychological, organic, and social factors that underlie his emotional problems.

TREATMENT: Including not only the modes of treatment, but the place of treatment. Hospitalization may be required.

Since most emotional illnesses can be considered, in the final analysis, to be both psychological and physiological in nature, it is not surprising that the means by which they are treated are both psychological and physical, and quite often both together. And so treatment divides into the organic therapies and the psychotherapies.

THE ORGANIC THERAPIES

Within the last twenty-five years a number of drugs have been discovered that significantly affect the symptoms and the course of the more severe mental illnesses, that is, the psychoses. The two most important classes of drugs are the major tranquilizers, which control anxiety and agitation, and the antidepressants. More recently lithium has been introduced for the treatment of manic states. These drugs are not curative. They are directed at the symptoms of illness rather than at its causes. Nevertheless, they are of such unmistakable value that there can be no excuse for withholding them in those circumstances where they are indicated: in the treatment of very disturbed patients. It must be noted, however, that these drugs, and also the minor tranquilizers, are sometimes given inappropriately as an excuse for avoiding a more painstaking treatment, or as a means of avoiding some of the difficulties involved in caring properly for a difficult person.

    *   *   *

A senile woman who lived in a nursing home was often frightened as the result of being confused; at such times she began to scream, which was distracting to the staff. Consequently they asked an attending psychiatrist to sedate her so that she would sleep during these periods—*although she was already sleeping twenty hours each day!* Medication used to such a purpose would have obliterated all signs of life!

No medicine can substitute for a careful attempt to meet a patient's real needs as they exist in the real world.

Electric shock treatment, another organic treatment, suggests to the lay person a cruel and dangerous punishment rather than a form of therapy. The fact is, however, that it is a safe and effective treatment for certain psychotic states, primarily depression. Every treatment in all of medicine is measured solely by that criterion: whether it achieves the desired effect without causing serious, or at least prohibitive, side effects. Nevertheless, the indications for electric shock treatment are narrowing as better medications are developed.

There are other organic therapies, including brain surgery, electro-sleep therapy, prolonged narcosis, carbon dioxide inhalation, and different forms of convulsive therapy. None of them has gained wide acceptance because none of them works very well.

PSYCHOTHERAPY

Although the organic therapies are prescribed only by a psychiatrist, psychotherapy is practiced in one form or another by everyone. It is an aspect of all relationships in which one person turns to another for comfort and for help, or for instruction. The goal of the psychotherapies is to help the patient see himself accurately and think well of himself, and to help him behave more effectively.

Insight Psychotherapy

Psychoanalysis and the various psychotherapies that have sprung from it consider self-understanding the essential goal of treatment. From insight come growth, mastery, self-control, and appreciation of self; from these comes freedom from illness. It is an old idea: examining one's life is essential to happiness. But it is plain that simply brooding does not lead to happiness, nor does it cure anything or anyone. A treating person, to whom the patient can relate, is still necessary. Indeed their relationship is the focus of treatment.

The patient and the therapist meet frequently, regularly, over a long period of time. The interchange in which they engage is a formal process governed by strict rules that have become so well-known that they are almost folklore. The therapist is dispassionate and restrained. He listens unprotestingly to whatever is said to him. He is patient. He hesitates to give concrete advice. He communicates as little as possible of his own attitudes and wishes. At the same time, he encourages the patient to fantasize, to talk about dreams, and, indeed, to say anything at all that occurs to him. The patient's reactions to the therapist are explored, since his behavior in the treatment setting illustrates those characterological defenses that he employs in his relationships with everyone else in his life. Finally, after a period of time the process of therapy and the therapist come to assume an important place in the patient's life: the patient becomes dependent on the therapist. Only after that period of secure dependence, which gives the patient courage to look at himself objectively, does he become truly independent. The job of therapy, then, is to explore and explain all of the patient's feelings and thoughts and all of his behavior.

Yet a patient does not really come to treatment to learn about himself, any more than he comes to learn how to behave differently. Invariably he resists developing insight or discovering anything about himself that may make him anxious.

Certainly he does not want simply to be told by his therapist what he has been told many times before by many different people: that his behavior is inappropriate or inadequate in some respect. He comes in order to feel better, and only after he is suffering somewhat less is he able to develop insight. He comes to be recognized in some way as an individual, and only then can he change.

Supportive Psychotherapy

Supportive psychotherapy is the attempt by a therapist by any practical means whatever to help a patient deal with his emotional distress and problems in living. It includes comforting, advising, encouraging, reassuring, and mostly listening, attentively and sympathetically. The therapist provides an emotional outlet, the chance for the patient to express himself and to be himself. Also the therapist may inform his patient about his illness and about how to manage it and how to adjust to it. Over the course of treatment he may have to intercede on the patient's behalf with various authorities, including schools and social agencies, and with the patient's family—indeed, with all of those with whom the patient may be contending. Often he must explain his patient's behavior to others; at the same time, he may have to interpret the meaning of other people's behavior to his patient. He must educate him to the unwritten but crucial rules that govern all social interaction. The therapist usually encourages his patient to expand his interests in the world by making friends, or by going to school or to work. He may encourage him to engage in sports or hobbies. To an extent, the therapist serves as a model for proper and appropriate behavior. The therapist conveys implicitly to the patient an ideology about the way that life ought to be led, as an independent, mature person.

Insight psychotherapy, then, is a formal, almost stylized, treatment directed solely at helping the patient to understand himself better. Supportive psychotherapy, on the other hand, is a varied attempt to help the patient deal with all the different problems attendant upon his emotional illness which in turn affect all the rest of his life.

There are other differences. Insight psychotherapy is an expensive, prestigious treatment conducted by a relatively few highly trained professionals, whereas supportive psychotherapy is conducted, in a skilled fashion or naively, by everyone who cares about the patient and is willing to care for him. The methods of these psychotherapies are different. The techniques of insight therapy include the interpretation of resistances, dreams, defense mechanisms, and transference reactions to the therapist. The process is prolonged. The supportive therapist deals more superficially, perhaps, but more immediately with the daily events of his patient's life. He appeals to the patient's conscious mind, rather than interpreting his unconscious. Also he is interested not only in what his patient tells him, which is the exclusive interest of the psychoanalyst, but in whatever else he can find out from the patient's family and friends, and from everyone else. Treatment may continue as long or longer than insight psychotherapy, at infrequent and irregular intervals; or it may be very intensive over only a short period of time. The indications for both treatments are also somewhat different. The patient deemed suitable for insight therapy is usually intelligent, motivated, relatively intact emotionally, and relatively well off financially, that is, able to afford the cost in time and money of treatment. Also such an ideal patient begins treatment, ideally, already inclined to thinking of himself in psychological terms. The patient for whom supportive therapy is recommended is likely to be poorer, less capable, and sicker, perhaps psychotic—less able to tolerate the anxiety of looking at himself objectively; but this need not be true. In order to benefit from a supportive psychotherapy, someone need not be sick to any particular degree, nor does he need to have any special kind of illness. He can be depressed or schizophrenic or sexually disturbed—or neurotic. He may be in crisis, or he may be chronically ill. He need have no special social or intellectual qualification, or impairment. He can be anyone.

Finally, the therapist himself behaves differently, depending on whether he regards himself as doing insight or supportive psychotherapy. In insight therapy he thinks twice before saying anything, and certainly before giving advice. In order not to prejudice the patient's remarks and attitudes, he tries to introduce as little of his own attitudes as possible. He strives toward anonymity. When he is doing supportive therapy, on the other hand, he is active and involved. Since his patient may be too disturbed to cope effectively by himself with his day-to-day problems, the therapist will give advice. He may hesitate to comment upon unconscious wishes and impulses lest he cause the patient to become still more anxious and disturbed, but he may speak openly in other ways. He may describe his own feelings toward the patient, if his purpose is to reassure. He may speak of his own life in order to demonstrate a point. In short, he can be himself.

As is usual in psychiatry, however, these distinctions blur in practice. There are times when a patient in insight psychotherapy requires active intervention and support from the therapist—and there are times when a very sick patient can and will accept certain insights into himself. No treatment of the emotionally disturbed can be applied as a formula. The distinction between these two idealized forms of psychotherapy is drawn here only to underline the fact that supportive therapy, at least, as it has been described here, is not exclusively in the hands of psychiatrists or psychologists but is conducted by others also. *Someone who lives with, or works with, an emotionally disturbed person is cast inevitably in the role of therapist.* If he actively cares for that person, he is conducting a supportive psychotherapy.

HOSPITAL TREATMENT VERSUS HOME TREATMENT

In the early days of civilization and for a very long time afterward, the mentally ill lived at home for the same reasons that everyone else lived at home: there was no place else to live. Certainly there were no institutions in which those so afflicted could be housed together and treated by a staff specially trained and specially committed to their care. But there came a time—in fact, different times in different places—when public note was taken of the neglect with which these unfortunate people were treated within their homes, and consequently facilities were built in which they could live together away from the stresses of life. Recently some compassionate persons have looked into the modern counterparts of these institutions and discovered to their surprise that the mentally ill who live there are still treated with neglect. And so, with the support of many psychiatrists, they have sought to close these institutions and return these patients to their communities and to their families! The fact is, the careless disregard that is usually the lot of those who are chronically and seriously ill mentally does not come from improper living arrangements but from improper care. Nevertheless it is true that there are certain times when a particular patient is better off in a hospital and other times when he is better off at home. Those considerations that are relevant in determining whether to hospitalize someone include the following:

1. The potential of a patient to commit suicide or to injure himself in some other way. In general, patients who are actively suicidal should be in the hospital, although it must be noted that patients not infrequently kill themselves even in that relatively protected setting, so that even there they need to be observed closely.

2. The potential of a patient to injure others. People have an

exaggerated conception of the potential of most psychotic patients to do violence; but some such patients do exist, and they should be admitted to a hospital for their own benefit as well as that of society.

3. The response that the patient has already shown to treatment. Hospitalization should be considered for a psychotic person who is unaware that he is sick, who does not cooperate in his treatment, or who has worsened despite treatment. Admission can serve as a signal to him and the people around him that something more needs to be done. Some patients need to be brought into a hospital simply to keep them away from substances of abuse such as alcohol or drugs.

4. The patient's need for treatments or tests that may be undertaken more easily within a hospital. Electric shock treatments, for example, are given more commonly and conveniently to someone as a hospital patient than as an outpatient.

5. The physical needs of the patient. Some patients need special diets or special programs of physical rehabilitation that can only be provided in a hospital. Some other patients need extra attention for physical illnesses, which may be both a cause and a consequence of a mental illness.

6. The merits of the particular hospital balanced against the alternative, which is usually the patient's home and family. Some hospitals are so awful—cruel and demeaning—that no one should be admitted to them. Yet some families are just as bad, and no one who is emotionally disturbed should be allowed to remain subject to their influence. Similarly the benefits of a good hospital must be measured against the benefits of a good family.

Ideally admission into a hospital brings the patient into a therapeutic community, every aspect of which is designed to have a beneficial effect upon him. He is protected from those influences in the outside world that have caused him to become ill. He is offered psychotherapy, individually and in groups; occupational therapy; recreational therapy; work therapy, perhaps; and the therapeutic attention of dozens of trained specialists. He is encouraged to express himself. He participates in decisions concerning his own treatment program. He receives as much medicine as he needs and no more. Although in a protected setting, he exerts himself to the limits of his ability. And so he becomes stronger.

Unfortunately in practice a hospital is a different sort of place. The presence of restraints, locked rooms, and locked wards suggests strongly to the patient that he is locked away not for his own benefit, but for the convenience of society. Upon admission he is cut off not only from the conflicts of ordinary life, but also from its supports. He sees his family infrequently and perhaps not at all. His letters and telephone calls may be limited or monitored. He can perform no real work. And rather than receiving special attention, he is likely to receive no attention at all: he may spend days or weeks with no more contact with staff than a perfunctory greeting in the morning.

The hospital patient is expected to conform to a stereotype of proper behavior that may not resemble at all the behavior of a normal person. He is supposed to be passive, agreeable, and above all quiet. He should not quarrel with staff or take issue with his physician. He should engage fully in the "treatment program," which means, among other things, confiding his private anxieties and anguish to strangers, some of whom are themselves emotionally disturbed. He is supposed to entertain himself by drawing pictures or watching television—and do these things always in concert with the other patients. He should not try to stay up later than everyone else or read a book when everyone else is taking a walk. Although he may have trouble controlling himself, that is precisely what he must do. He should not cling to the nurses, or violate their sanctuary, the nursing station. Certainly he must not express in action any sexual feelings that he may have.

All behavior of the patient, however reasonable, is likely, if inconvenient to the staff, to be explained as an aspect of deranged thinking. Even the commonplace urge to leave the hospital is interpreted in terms of the patient's inability to understand his condition or interpret reality. In this regard, a peculiar logic governs clinical decisions: a patient who wants very much to leave the hospital may be presumed to need further treatment, while a patient who wants to stay is presumed to have become too dependent, and is encouraged to leave. Sometimes there is no making sense out of medical judgments.

A twenty-two-year-old man was admitted to a well-known state hospital affiliated with a well-known medical school. The reasons for his admission were somewhat vague: "to give him a chance to pull his life together." He was told to expect to stay at least six months. Within only a few weeks, however, he found himself bored by the endless routine of hospital life, and he asked to be discharged. That was out of the question, he was told. He was too sick to leave the hospital. He left anyway that afternoon for a beer, returning, though, within the hour. In order to "set limits" for him, the doctors then transferred him to a locked ward. The patient, a vigorous man, responded to this punishment by determining once and for all to leave the hospital, if necessary against medical advice. This time he struck an attendant, took away the man's keys, and left. The police were called and with their help the patient was forcibly returned to the hospital a few hours later. He was placed in a locked room for the remainder of the day. Over the next month he escaped repeatedly and was recaptured each time until his psychiatrist, in exasperation, warned him that if he escaped one more time, he would not be permitted to reenter the hospital! The patient escaped forthwith and did very well during the next two years with no treatment whatever.

* * *

Of course, a mental hospital can be made to approach the ideal somewhat more closely. But even under the best of circumstances, hospitalization cannot by itself be regarded as a definitive solution to anyone's emotional problems. The less time spent in the hospital, the better. It is only an episode in the long-term course of an illness, and its principal purpose, therefore—besides coping with the acute phase of the illness—is to begin a course of treatment that will continue during the longer and more important period of aftercare.

There are advantages to conducting treatment in the patient's home when possible, rather than in the hospital or, for that matter, in the psychiatrist's office. The therapist who sees the patient in his home becomes something more than a functionary of a clinic or a social agency, more even than the knowledgable but aloof clinical specialist that is the facade of a psychiatrist or a psychologist. He becomes a real person and, to an extent, a guest. The patient, in turn, becomes a friend rather than a supplicant. Consequently, he is more willing to communicate openly. A home visit, which always takes time, is an unmistakable expression of interest to which the patient and particularly his family invariably respond. Family dynamics may be seen directly in the home instead of merely being inferred. Sometimes, even, the psychological causes of the patient's emotional disturbance can be seen and sometimes dealt with. Other members of the family who are present can be enlisted into the treatment process, and those who are emotionally disturbed, but not yet labeled as such, can receive special attention. Also the therapist learns by looking around him enough about the actual circumstances of his patient's life to avoid making recommendations that sound reasonable in theory but could never be implemented, for reasons that are plainly in view. For instance, a mother cannot be encouraged to spend more time by herself when she lives in two rooms with a family of six. A phobic patient cannot be encouraged to walk at night through the streets, if the streets of his neighborhood are very dangerous, and so on. Many psychotherapists find all sorts of reasons for not visiting a patient at home, but the real reason is that they are uncomfortable outside of the structured confines of their offices.

THE ROLE OF THE COLLATERAL THERAPIST

What then can a friend, supervisor, or counselor of some sort do to be helpful to a person who is emotionally or mentally ill? A number of things, depending on his relationship with the disturbed person and the nature of that particular illness. In each of the subsequent chapters a detailed account is given of the more serious emotional disturbances, and concrete suggestions are offered, but some of the more typical ways such a collateral therapist can be helpful are mentioned below. It must be understood that for conditions so serious, some professional person must be in overall charge of treatment, usually a psychiatrist or a psychologist. Any other helping person must act in concert with that primary therapist and under his direction.

1. *Attending the patient.* Emotionally disturbed people often feel a desperate loneliness which can be relieved to some extent by the presence of others. Having someone to listen carefully to them and sympathize is reassuring. Simply having another person nearby may be calming or comforting. The terrible sense of being worthless is dissipated somewhat by the knowledge that someone else cares.

2. *Gathering information about the patient.* The proper management of a mentally ill person depends on a detailed knowledge of his condition, but persons suffering from these illnesses tend not to be reliable informants. For example, alcoholics and drug abusers do not usually admit to the extent of their abuse of these substances. Psychotic persons especially

do not report their symptoms accurately. A patient may deny hearing voices while intermittently carrying on a conversation with the television set. For this reason information obtained by others close to the patient is important. A suicidal patient needs to be monitored especially closely.

3. *Motivating the patient*—to engage actively in treatment, and in life in general. Patients do not like to think of themselves as emotionally disturbed, which is the implication of being in treatment, so they leave treatment prematurely. Unfortunately, however, most psychiatric conditions are chronic and need attention even during the periods between acute exacerbations. Collateral therapists are helpful in ensuring that the patient continues in treatment and continues to take medicines when they are prescribed. Also their help is often crucial in ensuring that the patient participates in the social activities and other activities of daily living which are often part of a treatment plan.

4. *Interceding on the patient's behalf.* People who are emotionally disturbed are often in contention with others, such as school authorities, employers, police, representatives of various social agencies, and especially other members of their families. Consequently they need someone to intervene with these others on their behalf. Often a collateral therapist can make peace between everyone simply by listening to everyone. Also he may be able to assist a patient in obtaining welfare payments, or a lawyer, or a job, or any of a thousand things. Such simple, practical efforts often provide the margin that allows a patient to manage satisfactorily.

5. *Caring for the patient's physical health.* Certain emotional disorders cause profound effects on the physical well-being of patients. The collateral therapist may need to manage overt organic illnesses that grow out of emotional disorders and that, if neglected, tend to worsen and prolong those disorders. He may need to tend to the patient's personal hygiene, which otherwise might lapse into an unhealthy state.

And more. The ways people can be helpful to each other are innumerable and not easy to codify. But those inclined to that task take to it a special determination that makes them especially effective. By caring, they exert a special influence. This is a fact of significance, since psychotherapy is essentially the influencing of one person by another.

Of course, anyone who does psychotherapy, in any sense of the word, must be concerned with those same clinical issues that are of concern to a primary therapist doing treatment. He must be alert to his patient's personal reaction to him and to the response he has in return. Such a response is unavoidable, but it should be under control, to some extent measured. The therapist must be tolerant of the patient's weaknesses, but not indulgent. He must be sympathetic, but also dispassionate. He must be optimistic, but at the same time realistic. Finally he must have respect for the patient's symptoms. He must not expect too much improvement too fast. He must keep in mind especially that although he may intervene in his patient's life, he may not intrude. Considering these difficulties, it is remarkable that therapy works as well as it does, even in untrained hands.

THE ROLE OF THE FAMILY

Anyone who comes to know an emotionally disturbed person comes quickly to appreciate the influence that person's family has had on the development and course of his illness; but such an influence is just one aspect of the greater influence they have had on his overall development as a person, and on the course of his life. Therefore their effect on him is never simply good or bad, healthy or unhealthy, but diverse. The exercise, in which some people engage, of laying blame on parents for their children's troubles is futile, and worse—it is a source of more trouble. It may become a distraction from current problems. In any case it is a pointless burden for parents and other family members, who too often blame themselves anyway for the suffering of anyone among them who is emotionally ill. The guiltier they are made to feel, the more they draw back from the patient, often leaving him without support at a time when he is particularly vulnerable and most in need of it, and when, very often, he has no one else to rely upon.

The family is the principal resource of anyone who is emotionally disturbed—as it is the principal resource for anyone at all. It provides not only economic support, but every other kind of support, including usually warmth and friendliness, pleasure, and love. Family life is the principal social experience throughout life. The family is the matrix out of which each person grows. He comes to recognize himself as a person by seeing himself through the eyes of his family; he measures himself against their expectations. Often their aspirations for him become his own, and so become part of him forever.

Not surprisingly, someone who is emotionally or mentally ill usually first manifests signs of that illness at home with his family, although his behavior may not seem grossly abnormal. If he is a child or an adolescent, his symptoms may seem to be simply a delay of normal development. An adult may seem simply to be unhappy or worried. Or he may indeed show any of a wide range of unmistakable psychiatric symptoms, such as obsessions, phobias, delusions, and so on. Perhaps the most characteristic presentation of an emotional problem is the presence of self-defeating, maladaptive behaviors combined with an attitude toward oneself as being awful and unworthy. These feelings and those behaviors go hand in hand and explain each other. But they may not seem to be distinguishable in any special way from the rest of that individual's personality. For that reason they tend not to receive the attention they deserve at the appropriate time: early, before they have become fixed.

Another reason why a family may tend to overlook an emotional disturbance among its members is precisely because that disturbance does not usually appear discretely in only one of them, but rather exists *among* them, as a function of all of them. One person reacts to another, who reacts again to that first person or to someone else, and an arena of conflict develops. The person who is said to be ill may only be the one who is most disturbed, or perhaps simply the one most willing to be labeled as sick. Often in these circumstances the appropriate treatment is of the entire family. The goals of family treatment are to improve communication within the family so that everyone becomes aware of the feelings and concerns of all the others. Each person should understand his own role and how he fits in with all the others. The family must not be permitted to blame one person for the distress of all of them, and all of the family will have to make room for the eventual improvement of the one among them who is most obviously disturbed; for if they are determined to consider him sick, he will be condemned to playing out that role.

Because the patient's family are so close to him, they are in the best position to be helpful; yet, for just that reason, they may find being truly helpful difficult. They are too involved to be objective. They can listen sympathetically but not to all of the patient's thoughts and fantasies, not to his sexual thoughts, perhaps. Nor is the patient likely to express those thoughts comfortably to a member of his family. If a family member tries to intercede on the patient's behalf, that attempt may be resented as an intrusion. Even when someone can accept help gracefully from a therapist or from a friend, the same help coming from a member of his family seems to him to be demeaning. Similarly the therapist can point out to the patient aspects of his behavior that are inappropriate or undesirable, but a family member saying the same things might be accused of trying to mold the patient into his own image.

And yet it remains true that an interested, intact family is a tremendous asset in the treatment of any sort of emotional illness. They are with the patient most of the time. They know, without needing to inquire, how he feels and how he is spending his time. They know, usually before anyone else, whether he is improving or becoming worse. They are able to comfort him as no one else can, for they mean more to him. Their influence over him is tremendous, and he may try to become well for their sake. Of course, they can exert that influence imprudently by being arbitrary, perhaps, or selfish. Indeed, they can undermine treatment in all sorts of ways. But the natural inclination of families is not to interfere, but rather to help.

The family, every family, has a purpose as a social unit: it is to protect, to teach, to comfort, to allow dependence while encouraging independence—in short, to provide a setting in which maturation can occur. A good family encourages its members to behave in effective ways; yet it encourages them to find their own ways of behaving effectively. And such an effort is precisely the function of psychotherapy. Therefore, family members, at least some of them, come naturally to the tasks of psychotherapy.

THE EFFECTIVENESS OF PSYCHOTHERAPY

It is the conviction of most psychotherapists that their efforts have a significant effect. For one thing, patients report that they are being helped. However, clinical studies examining the benefits of psychotherapy have given ambiguous results. Some investigations seem to suggest that psychotherapy, even in the hands of a psychiatrist, is ineffective, judging, at least, from how well someone appears to be two or three years after seeking out treatment. Persons placed on a waiting list but never treated turn out to be as well adjusted as those who are! Other outcome studies, perhaps, are more encouraging. The fact is, though, all of these studies are misleading: the long-term influence of psychotherapy is simply too subtle to measure by current techniques in outcome studies. One might just as well try to determine the effect of four years of college by measuring the wisdom with which college graduates conduct their lives, and comparing it with that of high school graduates.

The immediate effect of psychotherapy is also important. Patients feel less anxious and less unhappy because they see a therapist. They are *comforted* by the process of psychotherapy, and that alone is sufficient justification for it. Psychotherapy is similar to the rest of medicine in this respect. For example, most childhood illnesses are self-limited, and consequently a group of children treated for certain conditions might be indistinguishable six months later from another group who had been similarly ill, but who had had no treatment; yet *while they were ill*, they might have felt much better by virtue of taking medicine to relieve their pain and discomfort, and by getting proper nursing care. Emotional illnesses are still more sensitive and more responsive to proper care. The results one might reasonably expect from a successful psychotherapy are as follows:

1. An immediate although perhaps modest relief of psychological pain and suffering.

2. A diminution of symptoms, in part because the patient is better able to adhere to other treatment regimens, including the use of drugs and other organic therapies.

3. An acceleration of the natural tendency of people to become well in time, and in certain chronic conditions, a slowing of the pathological process.

4. An avoidance of certain social catastrophes that acutely disturbed patients tend to visit upon themselves, such as the loss of a job, the dissipation of savings, the disruption of a family, and so on.

5. And certainly, in certain cases, the furtherance of a real growth of personality. The individual thinks better of himself and is better able to cope with stress and with the vicissitudes

of living. To a greater extent than before, he masters himself and his environment.

In such ways psychotherapy may have a crucial influence on someone who is emotionally disturbed—profoundly, if slowly, affecting both his attitudes and his behavior. As indicated throughout this chapter, it is not an easy treatment to do. Someone who is professionally trained over a period of years may find that years later he is still learning; yet it is not a technique of surgical precision, but rather a way of being with a patient—an attitude. Like anything else people do, it can be done well or less well, or poorly. For that reason, this book has been written. It is intended as a guide for those many people who by virtue of their work or their closeness to someone who is emotionally disturbed must care for such a person—and who have no other guide to help them.

3 PSYCHIATRIC EMERGENCIES

Most psychiatric illnesses, although diagnosed first during adult life, are thought to have their beginnings in childhood. They develop as the individual develops, over a period of years. Despite their early and slow onset, though, they often come first to medical attention, and to the attention of others, when they have provoked a crisis—suddenly. Apparently people are not inclined to pay attention to someone in emotional distress until that distress has become extreme. Even when that person has a history of previous emotional difficulty, he and his family soon forget that trouble until the next time he must come for treatment, after his condition has deteriorated to the point where he is once again in crisis.

A *crisis* may be defined as a state of upset of equilibrium caused either by the individual's decreased ability to cope with the usual stresses of his life or by the introduction into his life of an unusual stress so severe that it is beyond his ability to cope. Not only tragic events but a seemingly happy event such as the birth of a child or a promotion may trigger an emotional reaction. Different people are upset by different experiences, each of them to a different degree. Sometimes patients come to treatment in an emotional crisis that has no obvious cause. In general the less obvious and less extraordinary the circumstances to which the person is responding, the more likely he is to have a significant, underlying emotional disorder. Conversely, someone who breaks down only in the face of overwhelming stress may well have been, and may continue to be in the future, a relatively well-adjusted person. Still, at the time of crisis he may be quite disturbed.

Crises are dramatic in onset. The individual comes to treatment—or is brought to treatment by his family—following an upheaval of some sort. He may have made a suicide attempt, or a threat of suicide. Or he may have become violent or shown evidence of other dangerous or inappropriate behavior. He may have provoked a sudden marital conflict. Or he may simply be behaving in some, for him, uncharacteristic manner recognizable in some way as abnormal. He may have trouble eating and sleeping, or he may have other physical symptoms. He may be anxious or agitated or depressed or confused. The fact is, he may demonstrate any symptom at all of emotional distress.

Such emotional turmoil has two major consequences over and above the immediate discomfort it causes:

The individual becomes vulnerable to additional stress and therefore is in danger, at least under certain circumstances, of becoming chronically, and more profoundly disturbed.

Yet, at the same time, he becomes particularly amenable to change. In the midst of suffering, he is motivated, as he may not have been previously, to examine himself and to find better ways of coping.

In short a crisis represents not only the danger of a severe disruption of personality, but also an opportunity for growth. Treatment, of course, is directed at preventing one and furthering the other.

CRISIS INTERVENTION

In the management of crisis, treatment must be intensive and immediate. The patient should be seen frequently. His family also should be seen and involved in the process of treatment, and, if appropriate, so should others, such as his employer, perhaps, or his pastor, or friends. *A lot of effort expended quickly is much more effective than much more effort expended later on.* At the height of crisis the patient is willing to reach out for help; but within only a few days he may have withdrawn, or he may have become too regressed or too sick to respond well. Or he may have precipitated such a storm by behaving in a dangerous or undesirable fashion that he will have to be hospitalized. Indeed he may have killed himself and put himself forever beyond help.

Treatment begins with an attempt to identify the stress to which the patient is presumably responding. Such a process of evaluation is equivalent to making a diagnosis.

In order to conclude reasonably that an event, or combination of events or circumstances, is the cause of an emotional crisis, it should not only have happened recently, but it should be prominent in the patient's concerns. The areas in life that are most likely to generate stress, and that should be searched especially, are those that at other times provide most of life's satisfactions. These include the patient's work and his relationships with his family and friends. Financial difficulties and physical illness are other common sources of anxiety. On close examination the patient will be found often to be responding to a loss of some sort or to a real or symbolic threat.

The patient's reaction to these significant circumstances, whichever they happen to be, should be understandable in terms of his past life and his personality. His therapist should therefore know enough about him to determine why those particular circumstances are stressful. For that reason a proper interest must be shown in the patient's relevant past, even though his distress is in the present and of recent onset. The attempt to understand his distress is itself a significant first step in treatment, for it communicates two ideas: that the patient is worth paying attention to and that his problems are in principle comprehensible and therefore solvable.

In order to explore fully the patient's feelings and thoughts, the therapist should be warm and supportive, able to listen calmly to his worries and fears without becoming frightened himself, yet willing to take those fears seriously. If the patient feels guilty or angry for some seemingly strange or foolish reason, those feelings too should be addressed. It may be possible to indicate to the patient some plan—even some very preliminary plan—to deal with his problems. If he feels threatened, some measures should be taken to make him feel secure. If he feels bereft, some reasonable hope should be held out to him that his loss may be compensated. Often, common-sense observations are helpful. The therapist may be in the position to intervene directly in the patient's life to diminish the stress to which he is responding. This must be done cautiously and respectfully, so as not to undermine the patient's ability to act in his own behalf.

Some persons in crisis, if they are very anxious or depressed, may need medication. Some others may need the special facilities of a hospital. But all will have needs of one sort or another that must be met by whoever is caring for them, if they are to get well. Usually in time, and with some help, the patient can learn his own effective ways of coping with his problems.

Although any psychiatric condition can present as an emergency, those that carry with them the threat of violence are the most serious. The following sections—the Violent Person, the Child Abuser, the Suicidal Person—illustrate the principles of crisis intervention in the context of these particular conditions.

THE VIOLENT PERSON

Violence is extremely common, violent crimes occurring literally in the hundreds of thousands every year. Individuals assault each other impulsively, almost casually, even those whom they love. The causes of violence are, consequently, the subject of much attention. Every time someone commits a violent act so egregious that it comes to public notice, a dozen reasons are given for it and for all acts of violence. Poverty is blamed, or prejudice, or overcrowding. But the truth is that the causes of violence are innumerable.

Mental illness is commonly alleged to be a principal cause for violent behavior; for that reason many uninformed people are frightened of someone who is obviously disturbed emotionally. Yet mental illness, like most physical illness, tends to impair the individual's ability to act, aggressively or in any other way. Only a few such conditions have a significant potential to precipitate a violent act. Among these is paranoid schizophrenia, which may affect the individual so that he comes to believe that people are persecuting him. He may then attack whomever he imagines his enemies to be. Certain drugs—for example, amphetamines—produce psychotic paranoid states which can be dangerous for the same reason. As everyone knows, alcoholic intoxication, because it lowers impulse control, causes some people to become violent; if they are chronic alcoholics, they become violent over and over again. Certain rare forms of epilepsy and other confusional states that sometimes occur as a complication of organic disease may cause the individual to strike out indiscriminately at whoever is nearby; but since these attacks are unpremeditated and uncoordinated, they do not often result in someone being injured. Occasionally, sexually deviant individuals become notorious by committing sadistic or murderous acts, but these too are unusual and represent the behavior of only a tiny fraction of those who are sexually disturbed or deviant. There are in addition certain very dangerous, very strange, hysterical psychoses—such as amok—which stimulate the individual to sudden and usually short-lived bouts of murder, but these are exceedingly rare. And there are still other people who are labeled with a psychiatric diagnosis, such as explosive personality, precisely because they are repeatedly violent, irrationally and with little provocation; such a term signifies nothing at all about them beyond the fact that they are indeed violent. Certainly they are not psychotic, or mentally ill in any conventional sense. It is true, of course, that any psychotic or neurotic person can commit a violent act, but only because *any person at all can commit such an act*. The fact is that violence is an uncommon complication of mental illness.

Some attempts have been made to predict who will become violent, and who having once been violent, perhaps criminally violent, will become violent again. Not much success has been achieved. Psychiatrists, who are often charged legally with the responsibility for saying whether someone is dangerous, are often wrong. What is not commonly appreciated is that they are likely to exaggerate the danger rather than minimize it. They are more likely to hold patients indefinitely in a hospital on the sometimes arbitrary presumption of their dangerousness than they are to release homicidal persons into the community carelessly, as they are often accused of doing.

The indicators, such as they are, by which a person's potential for violence is judged, are as follows:

1. A previous history of violence. The more frequent and vicious someone's past violent acts, the more likely he is to be violent again. Often adults who have committed crimes of violence give a long history of other similar acts, dating back to their childhood. They may have had difficulty in school be-

cause of fighting; or they may have exhibited an odd triad of symptoms: bed-wetting, fire-setting, and cruelty to animals. Probably any cruelty or wanton destructiveness is a sign of a defect of personality which may manifest itself at some point in the willful injury of others.*

2. Menacing behavior. Someone who threatens violence when he is angry, or who punches walls or breaks furniture, or who in some other way shows poor impulse control, is likely to strike out at someone when he is particularly angry. Similarly, someone who nurses a grievance and constructs plans for revenge may undertake some day to consummate those plans. Threats are sometimes a prelude to an overt act. Threats can be expressed also nonverbally, through the individual's demeanor. Some people, before losing control, give warning by quarreling and shouting and by becoming agitated—in short, by appearing as if they are about to lose control. And some people, of course, openly state their intention of committing a violent act.

3. A pattern of engaging in activities where violent encounters are likely to occur. Certain social settings undermine the usual strictures against violence. For instance, someone in a rioting mob is capable of perpetrating a violent act even though ordinarily he is in good control of himself. Similarly, a person who frequents bars constantly or who associates with drug addicts places himself in a setting where violent behavior is tacitly encouraged because it is construed as a sign of manliness; consequently, this person may learn to be violent. Such learning occurs also in certain families so consumed by rage that their members repeatedly attack each other physically. Merely living with such a family is an incitement to violence.

As people become violent for different reasons, they are also violent in different ways:

*The petty vandalism of adolescents in groups does not have this implication.

One man became drunk regularly and punched his wife and children when he came home. On one occasion, his wife, presumably in a spirit of self-defense, stabbed him with a kitchen knife, precipitating the need for an emergency operation in order to save his life.

Another man, after a fight with his father, went to a park where he raped the first woman he saw.

Another man, when he became angry at his wife, shot a rifle out of his window at passing cars.

A woman who had had no previous history of violent or abnormal behavior became so desperate upon delivering an illegitimate child that she killed it by throwing it into an incinerator.

A twelve-year-old boy kicked his younger siblings at every opportunity and finally killed one of them with a hammer.

These examples could be multiplied endlessly. The variety of violence is extraordinary. The attendant risk to others depends on the strength and the intent of the violent impulse, the circumstances under which it arises, and the response of those people who are immediately present.

Treatment

The violent person is usually violent again and again; therefore proper treatment must extend past the moment of violence itself and over a period of time. The therapist—who in this case may be almost anyone, a parole officer perhaps, or even a lawyer—must accomplish with this difficult patient the basic goals of any therapy. He must establish a trusting relationship between them in which the patient can express frustration verbally instead of by striking out. Indeed, they must be able to discuss openly not only the patient's violence but all of his behavior.

Obviously the first principle of managing someone potentially violent is to see to it, as far as possible, that he does not in fact injure anyone, for his own sake as well as for everyone else's. The knowledge of having harmed another human being is terribly destructive to self-respect. Consequently, if it seems that there is a real risk of someone becoming violent, the police or other legal authorities should be involved without hesitation at a time when they can prevent his actions rather than punish them. Some people, rather than call the police, play out the role of victim over and over. By being so passive, or perhaps masochistic, they may actually provoke attacks upon themselves. *No one should subject himself, or herself, to repeated physical assaults—or allow others to be subjected to them.* Surprisingly some people refuse to take the dangerousness of physical attack seriously, especially if they are not themselves a victim.

An army corporal was sent for psychiatric examination after he was found choking another soldier in the bathroom of his barracks. It was the third such assault he had committed that month, each time on a different person. Each time, the attack was interrupted fortuitously by other personnel who happened to walk into the room. The only explanation the corporal gave for these attacks was that these individuals "did not deserve to live," and so he set out to kill them. There was no particular reason why they were undeserving of life. In fact when pressed, the corporal went so far as to admit that so far, at the age of nineteen, he had not yet come across anyone who in his judgment deserved to live.

His life before he entered the army was one violent incident after another. When he was small, he tortured and killed little animals, then larger animals when he was older. He committed petty larceny at an early age, then graduated to armed robbery and assault with a deadly weapon. He attacked members of his own family, once with a wrench. From the time he was ten, his family refused to allow him in the house, and he lived thereafter in different foster homes and then different reformatories, one after another. Finally, when he was eighteen years old, a judge who found him guilty of assault gave him the choice of serving a jail sentence or of enlisting in the army. He chose to enlist.

The psychiatrist contacted the corporal's commanding officer and asked why the corporal, who was so obviously dangerous, had not been discharged from the service following the first of these three serious assaults. "Because he's the best gunner I have," replied the captain unabashedly. The fact that the United States happened to be at peace at the time made no difference. Taken aback, the psychiatrist asked the captain what it would take to convince him that the corporal was potentially homicidal. "Only if he killed someone," the captain said. "Anyone who really wants to kill someone has no trouble doing it."

The corporal was discharged from the service on psychiatric grounds before this provocative theory could be put to the test.

Violent behavior should never be overlooked, for it is an indicator of more violence to come.

Those few who are violent and who are mentally ill by conventional criteria should be distinguished from those others who are simply violent. Someone truly ill should receive proper medical care, in a hospital if he is psychotic. If he becomes assaultive there, he may need to be restrained still further by placing him in a seclusion room or by the use of medication. For those individuals who are not obviously ill mentally, but who are repeatedly violent nevertheless, even jail, which teaches nothing, is preferable as a last resort to allowing such a pattern to continue.

Two commonsense precautions may prevent recurrent episodes of violent behavior in someone with such a history and will minimize their danger when they do occur:

1. No weapons should be kept about the house or be immediately accessible. The presence of a gun *suggests* violence and can transform a simple family dispute into murder. Statistically these weapons represent a hazard to their owners more serious than any conceivable danger from intruders. Husbands and wives shoot each other accidentally, and on purpose, in great numbers.

2. The violent person should be encouraged to stay away from situations in which he previously has been unable to control his aggressive impulses. He may have to stay out of bars or away from certain neighborhoods—perhaps even away from certain members of his family. When, despite these precautions, he begins to show premonitory signs of losing control of himself, the people around him should intervene before it is too late. Often he will give evidence of increasing emotional distress before striking out, by becoming sullen or agitated or threatening, and there is still time then to reason with him.

The Moment of Violence

Whatever the roots of violent behavior, the violent act itself is usually precipitated immediately by a powerful emotion, rage or fear; these feelings, in turn, grow out of a sense of frustration or helplessness. Anyone who has the misfortune to confront the violent person in the midst of an outburst would be well advised, therefore, not to do anything likely to make him feel more frustrated or helpless. It is unwise to challenge him or defy him or show contempt for him. He may be prodded over the threshold of overt violent action by any strong display of feeling on the part of someone confronting him. For that reason that person, however difficult the circumstances, should try not to become angry or panicky. He should sit quietly, if he can, and listen. Even in these moments of crisis the beginnings of a relationship can form, or if such a relationship already exists, it can be appealed to. Someone paying close attention and trying to help has a calming influence. As soon as the violent person is talking rather than acting, the danger of his hurting someone is greatly diminished.

No one should undertake to disarm someone holding a weapon. No one should tackle such a person or sneak up behind him. Particularly, no one should turn his back and simply walk away or run away. These behaviors seem to be an invitation to an attack. Similarly, one should not merely pretend that there is no danger. Surprisingly, some people respond to danger with unconcern, to the point sometimes of going to sleep while being threatened with a pistol! Such a blithe indifference to the feelings and actions of the person threatening violence is inappropriate and may provoke him into commanding attention by committing a destructive act that he might never have intended and that he might not otherwise have done.

If someone is agitated and threatening but not armed with a weapon, he is, of course, less dangerous; but he may still be very frightening to the people around him. If they are afraid for their own safety, they will find it hard working effectively to calm him. The best thing, then, is to leave if leaving is feasible. If someone feels that he is in an acute and immediate danger, he must think of himself first. He should return only when there are enough people with him to make him feel safe and to indicate to the violent person that any physical outburst on his part would be quickly subdued. Usually under those circumstances even a very agitated person will not attack. If restraints are necessary, as they are sometimes, these too should be sufficiently powerful to discourage resistance and struggle. They must be applied correctly. Handcuffs, a straitjacket, or any other restraint applied improperly is unsafe to the person being restrained and to the people around him.

Unfortunately there are disadvantages to calling the police. The presence of a policeman often seems to represent a challenge to someone who is already inclined to fight. If the police must be called—and especially if they are called to subdue an agitated, aggressive, and mentally ill patient—they should leave their weapons somewhere else. In a scuffle the patient may seize a pistol from a policeman with the result that a gunfight ensues; such unpleasant scenes are not unusual in the emergency rooms of psychiatric hospitals.

Once the moment of violence has passed, a stubborn effort should be made to involve the individual in a program of intensive treatment. Every modality of treatment has been reported to have some success, including group and individual psychotherapy. If the violent behavior is focused within the family, conjoint family therapy probably offers the best chance of resolving the conflicts that underlie such behavior. In the last analysis, however, fundamental to any method of treatment is the relationship formed between the patient and the therapist. Some violent individuals are so resentful or frightened that they are distrustful of anyone who offers to help them. But they may be even more frightened by their own loss of control, so that during the immediate aftermath of a violent episode, they become amenable to treatment. During this crisis period, they should have ready access to the therapist, if necessary by telephone. They must have the opportunity to talk about their aggressive impulses, rather than act upon them. In a way the therapist interposes himself between the patient and his violent nature. Because it is plain that the therapist is trying to help, it is rare for him to become himself the object of that violence.

The violent person is a problem to society and to himself. Often his destructive urges are turned against himself. He may mutilate himself or commit suicide. Insofar as he hurts others, he hurts himself. Unfortunately, because he is frightening to others, he is often turned away from conventional treatment centers until finally he has committed a violent act so serious that it results in his being incarcerated, perhaps for the rest of his life. And yet he is not beyond help.

CHILD ABUSE

An especially awful form of violence is the brutal, physical attack that some parents make upon their own children, to the point sometimes of killing them. One might think that such acts are rare, and that parents capable of them must necessarily be psychotic, but the facts are otherwise. Gross physical abuse is inflicted on thousands, perhaps hundreds of thousands, of infants and children every year in this country by parents who may seem, at least at first glance, to be perfectly normal. The greater number of these children are very young, but children of any age can become victims. As the result of these attacks, many are crippled permanently, both physically and mentally. Approximately one third become mentally retarded. And it is possible that as many as twenty to twenty-five percent of these children are killed eventually at the hands of their parents, more than the number who die as the result of the common childhood diseases. Perhaps the strangest aspect of this strange clinical syndrome is that the parents of these children usually love them.

Child abuse is defined customarily as a deliberate physical attack by a parent on his child, resulting in an injury to the child. These attacks, although irrational, are not without pattern or without meaning. Most cases of child abuse bear a surprising resemblance to each other. The following case history, although seemingly extraordinary, is typical.

Betty, who was just three years old, was brought to the emergency room of a general hospital by her parents for treatment of injuries that were sustained, according to their account, when she fell down a flight of stairs. She had received no prior medical attention, although the incident had occurred twelve hours previously.

While Betty's parents spoke to the physician, she sat quietly alongside them, dressed, as they were, very properly and primly. When she was asked how she felt, she replied politely, "Fine." When she was examined, however, she began to cry softly. Obviously she was in pain, but surprisingly, she made no effort to cling to her parents or to turn to them for comfort. Examination revealed that her injuries were not compatible with having fallen downstairs. She had burn marks on her back, some of which were old, and she had distinctive loop-shaped bruises and lacerations on her abdomen and across her back. These wounds were recognized immediately as having resulted from her being struck with a lamp cord or a similar small rope. Her principal injury, however, was a broken wrist. Further X-ray examinations revealed evidence of a number of previous, partially healed fractures, including fractures of both arms and both legs. It was plain that Betty was a battered child. She had been physically abused, severely and repeatedly.

Betty's parents agreed hesitantly to her being hospitalized for further tests, whereupon a clinical investigation was begun to determine the full extent of her injuries and, at the same time, determine the social and psychological circumstances at home that had led to her being abused. Except for her obvious injuries, she seemed to be normal physically. Her behavior, however, could not be described as normal. She smiled pleasantly and superficially at everyone but seemed to relate closely to no one. Much of the time she seemed frightened and withdrawn. Her parents were also withdrawn and uncommunicative; it was only over a period of weeks and months of regular home visits by a team of social workers and psychiatrists whom they came slowly to trust that the facts of Betty's relationship with them emerged.

Betty's mother was a young woman who when she was

small had herself been beaten cruelly by her own mother. She grew up resenting her mother, but was dependent on her for approval, which she seemed never to receive. Consequently she had little self-respect. Her relationships with others were similarly ambivalent. She wanted people to like her, yet she withdrew from them. She trusted hardly anyone, including her husband. Most of the time she was lonely and depressed. When she was frustrated, she behaved impulsively; and on certain occasions, when she was angry at Betty, she found herself, almost unawares, grabbing the child by a limb and flinging her full force against a wall. Although she recognized that this behavior was abnormal, and although she knew that she had other emotional problems as well as marital problems, she had never gone to anyone for help.

Her husband came from a similar background. Although he had not been beaten as a child, neither had he experienced any tenderness. His parents disliked him. Probably as a result, he grew up to be an unfriendly, unsympathetic man. He was impatient with his wife and given to sulking. At those times when she was unable to manage the children successfully, he was likely to storm out of the house and stay away for a day or two. Although he disapproved in general with her ways of caring for their children, he never offered to help.

There were two children born of this union, and both had been physically abused by their mother. George was eight years old. He was a very quiet, very cooperative child, according to school authorities. They noted with surprise, therefore, that he had frequently been punished severely by his parents. On three occasions he had been sent to the school nurse for treatment of bruises and lacerations which they suspected were the result of beatings, although he said each time in explanation that he had fallen off a chair or down a flight of stairs. He had missed a number of months of school with the excuse that he had been ill. Yet his medical records, when they were collected from various physicians and hospitals, revealed a consistent pattern of physical abuse and torture. At twelve months of age he had sustained burns on the buttocks which had resulted from his mother's placing him on a hot stove, "to teach him not to wet himself," she explained subsequently. Apparently from the time he was two, he was burned repeatedly with lighted cigarettes as a way of punishing him for being messy. He was beaten with a cord for wetting his bed at night. Once after having accidentally knocked over a lamp, he was beaten so severely that he was hospitalized with a broken arm and a fractured skull. At the age of eight he showed some evidence of permanent brain damage as the cumulative result of this mistreatment.

Betty, who was an unwanted, premature baby, was treated still worse. From the time she was six months of age, she was placed on a rigid program of toilet training, which was enforced by whippings. Fortunately she was completely trained by the age of ten months. She was still punished, however, for any deviation from her mother's conception of how a good child should behave. She was burned with lighted cigarettes for crying; once, because she refused to eat everything on her plate, her mother bit her.

The attack on Betty that finally brought the family to the attention of a psychiatrist was typical of a dozen others that had occurred previously. Betty's mother had had an argument with her husband, who had complained about her inability to keep the children's room clean and neat. When she pointed out that a storm the previous day had broken one of the windows and caused damage in the room, he yelled back that he was fed up with her excuses. He packed a small bag and left immediately, without saying another word. Betty called to him from the doorway and began to cry; whereupon her mother began to beat her and finally threw her bodily across the room. The only explanation the mother could give later for her behavior, which she only vaguely remembered, was that she was angry at her daughter's endless complaining and "her sexual advances toward her father."

Perhaps the most remarkable aspect of this case is that a number of physicians, teachers, and other professional persons had reason to know, or at least suspect, that these children were being brutalized, yet they did nothing to intervene.

These, then, are the significant features of this family which are typical of such cases:

1. The parents had little self-respect or self-confidence. Consequently they isolated themselves. They were inept when they were forced to deal with other people. They could be described also as immature, impulsive, and unreliable. Although they depended excessively on each other, they could not trust each other or anyone else. None of these weaknesses, however, would have resulted in child abuse had not both parents also demonstrated a defect in empathy, in the ability to feel what other people, especially their children, were feeling.

2. When they were children, both parents suffered from their parents' overwhelming disapproval; sometimes this disapproval took the form of overt physical abuse. Even when they were grown up, their parents treated them without respect, as if they were, even then, children who were unsatisfactory somehow and incompetent. In order to get along at all with their parents, they had to submit completely to their judgment and to their wishes.

3. The abusing parents, almost surely as the result of their own childhood experiences, had a distorted conception of the proper relationship between a parent and a child. They seemed to feel that a child exists in order to satisfy its parents' needs, to comfort them. A crying child was someone who was scolding and rejecting—and bad. Their ideas about the developing capacities of a child were similarly absurd. An infant of six months of age was supposed to be capable of bladder con-

trol. A two-year-old was expected to remain clean. Any inability to live up to these unreasonable expectations was regarded as a willful failure. And just as a child was expected to have the virtues of an adult, he might also be suspected of having an adult's vices—and so a three-year-old was thought to be wanton.

4. The physical attack itself occurs immediately in response to an emotional stress. Those situations that are particularly distressing to abusing parents are any that seem to suggest an abandonment or rejection. But even ordinary frustrations can provoke an assault. Often the parent is in the midst of caring for his child when he is provoked into a murderous rage by the child's clumsiness or uncooperativeness.

In sum, the causes of child abuse might be said to be the combination of these circumstances: a parent who has grown up with the experience of disapproval and violence, a lonely marriage that offers neither parent support nor comfort, and a precipitating emotional stress. And, of course, the presence of a child.

Unfortunately such abuse is allowed to occur usually until the child is beaten so severely that his injuries can no longer escape notice. By then his physical health, and, of course, his emotional health, may be permanently damaged. Only at that point when his condition is critical are people likely to recognize that a crisis exists within his family. Even then the reaction of hospitals, schools, social agencies, courts, and all the other appendages of society is often inadequate or worse, irrelevant. For example, a fine of a hundred dollars is not likely to deter a parent who assaults his children or help him with those serious emotional problems from which he suffers and which work to endanger his child.

In order to prevent the inevitable consequences of continued child abuse—which may persist in one family from generation to generation—therapeutic intervention must take place energetically as soon as possible. Many different resources of the community must be involved, and those individuals who are willing to be involved personally in the therapeutic processes must give their own resources unstintingly.

Diagnosis

No physician likes to think that the child he is examining has been deliberately injured by his parents, but once that possibility has occurred to him, he usually has little difficulty in making a definitive diagnosis. The pattern of abuse is recognizable. Typically, parents are reluctant to give an account of their child's injury, or they may give varying accounts. Whatever these explanations are, they are not usually consistent with the physical findings. A further indication of abuse is evidence of delay in seeking medical attention. The parents may seem unconcerned by the extent of the child's injury. There may be a history from other members of the family, or from neighbors, of numerous previous injuries. X-ray examinations can reliably distinguish these injuries from others which are caused accidentally. And there may be signs, even in the doctor's office, of family discord. A parent may be missing, or if both parents are present, they may sit apart and not speak to each other. Their child, although injured, may not turn to them for comfort.

Care of the Child

An appropriate first step in the care of the child is admission into a hospital. Observation to rule out intracranial and intraabdominal bleeding is always indicated, since these are frequent complications of abuse. A psychological evaluation of the child should be made and treatment of the child's physical and emotional problems started at once. In order to protect the child from further abuse, he should not be returned home, even at the demand of his parents, until it is plain that he will be safe in their care. Once he is returned home, he will still need to be followed carefully in order to continue treatment and make sure that no further abuse occurs.

Care of the Parents

Concurrent with the evaluation of the child in the hospital should be an evaluation of his family at home. A professional team of at least two or three members—which may include a pediatrician, a psychiatrist, a social worker, a nurse, or a child-welfare worker—should visit the family regularly with two purposes in mind: first, to determine as accurately as possible the sum of that family's life together; and second, to establish a therapeutic relationship with both parents. In order to achieve both purposes the parents should be approached respectfully and honestly. Any attempt to interrogate them with the intent of laying blame will only reinforce their sense of worthlessness and drive them away. They are likely, in any case, to resist treatment, since they have learned not to expect anyone's approval or help. Often such parents must be pursued patiently and stubbornly over a period of months before they will come to trust anyone who is trying to help them. And yet almost always they do want to be helped.

The parents should know that they are at the center of treatment just as much as their child is; but they should understand also that their child cannot be sacrificed to them. Inevitably the therapeutic team must decide whether and when the child should be returned home. When this responsibility is exercised with due concern, the parents will usually agree. Often they will object to a child being removed from their care, only to volunteer later on that they really understood at the time that it was the right decision.

A therapeutic team is necessary because the emotional needs of these parents are too great usually to be satisfied by one person. Someone must be available to them all of the time, day and night, at least by telephone—to listen to them if they are home alone, to reassure them, to encourage them, and to provide them some opportunity to express themselves in words rather than by assaulting their children. Neighbors who are truly interested, and distant members of the family who care, can be very helpful. Because abusive parents have suffered real deprivation, they need someone at this critical point in their lives to be especially giving and accepting of them, yet they are not easy people to like. The therapist must find within himself the grace to care about them, despite their abuse of children, an act repugnant to everyone. Sometimes a therapist has to sit by uncomfortably, but uncritically nevertheless, while a parent treats a child harshly or unfairly. The therapist must convince himself that the child's long-range interests are best served by his not rising to his defense too quickly or too often, at least before he has established a firm relationship with the parents. These parents do not come to treatment usually at their own request, and so they are less willing to put up with criticism or with any of the other very real discomforts of therapy. Of course if a parent is being dangerously brutal to his child, no one can stand by dispassionately. Usually at that point, however, the child is best protected by removing him from his home. The therapist's concern for the child need not then interfere with his treatment of the parents.

The therapist should not only refrain from being critical of these parents, he should help them become less vulnerable to the criticism of others. They should not have to live up to the excessively rigid standards of their own parents, or for that matter, to the standards of anyone else. Of course, they must take good care of their children; but with only modest guidance they can choose their own ways of being a proper parent and of living properly. Certainly the therapist should not give out a whole new set of rules for them to obey slavishly and resentfully.

Perhaps the single aim of the therapist during the first few weeks is to make friends with these friendless people. Such a relationship becomes possible if their passivity and resistance to treatment can be overcome. It is a friendship that will be tested frequently—and probably can never formally come to an end. They must have someone to rely on all of the time. If they turn safely to the therapist, or to the therapeutic team, for support, they will not lean on their children, who cannot possibly satisfy them or sustain them. The focus of treatment then is on the abusing parent—not on his management of his children exclusively, or even primarily—but rather on him, himself, or, more properly, on him and her, for both parents need help. Their needs must be met before they in turn can meet the needs of their child.

All such parents have certain needs in common.

Because their social functioning is impaired, they need encouragement and guidance in dealing with other people. They may need someone to intercede between them and others, especially between them and their own parents. And they need to make friends.

Because their self-control is poor, they need help in devising ways of responding to stress other than by striking out physically. As they become more resourceful, they are less threatened by anything that goes wrong, and also less frustrated.

Because they are ignorant of the way children ordinarily behave, they should be educated in normal child development. Ultimately, they should be helped to see their child as an individual with his own special needs and feelings.

Finally, because the symptom of child abuse does not disappear immediately in response to treatment, the abusing parent must have someone into whose care he can place the child from time to time, at least for a few hours. This person can be a family member, a homemaker, a public health nurse, a foster grandparent, or simply a baby-sitter. Such help should not be offered grudgingly. Even if a parent seems to want to be rid of his child for no apparent good reason, he should have that opportunity, for his and his child's sakes.

Goals of Treatment

Removing a child from the home of abusing parents is not a final solution to his or his parents' problems. Too often he is left then in the care of his grandparents, who are likely to be ill-suited themselves to bring up children. Other more distant members of the family may be able to help temporarily by caring for the child, but not usually for any length of time. And foster homes, when they are available, are rarely adequate. Even if the child stays for a while in a hospital or with some other member of his family or in a foster home, he is almost always sent back sooner or later to live with his parents, whether they are any better able to take care of him by then, or not. The central goal of treatment, therefore, is to help the parents learn how to care for their child effectively and safely, since responsibility for his care will surely rest with them in the long run.

But treatment should serve other purposes as well. The entire family should become more effective—as a family. They should be able to communicate with each other and to satisfy each other's needs. They should develop the skills to deal with the inevitable conflicts and crises that are part of life. Both parents and children should be able to enjoy each other as individuals. And each of them should have friends and a satisfying life outside of the family. Even by these relatively high standards, the treatment of child abuse, when it is immediate and intensive, is successful in most cases. Considering the stakes involved for these children, no justification is possible for offering less than the very best treatment.

Prevention

Much can be done to prevent child abuse, including the following measures:

1. Education in the proper care of children and in child development. Such information should be common knowledge and certainly should be made available systematically to women who are about to become mothers.

2. Family planning. Someone who does not want children may not be a good parent. Young people should know about contraception, and women should have easy access, if necessary, to proper facilities for an abortion.

3. Adherence to laws requiring physicians and others to report suspected cases of child abuse. The numbers of reported cases are growing rapidly. Ideally a central registry of abusing parents should be maintained somewhere, since these families frequently move from one place and from one jurisdiction to another.

4. Early case finding. Interviews and questionnaires are able to select out ahead of time women who are likely to become abusing mothers. When the ideas of such women are explored, they demonstrate a poor understanding of expectable child behavior and a belief in strict corporal punishment as essential to proper child rearing. Also it can be determined readily whether these women have had the sort of upbringing typically associated with this condition.

5. Proper postnatal care. Mothers should have contact with their newborn children as soon as possible. A significant percentage of abused children were born prematurely and consequently were kept away from their mothers for a number of days or weeks afterward. There is evidence that such a separation may weaken the tie between mother and child, perhaps permanently.

Child abuse is perhaps only one extreme on a continuum that includes the neglect of children by certain parents and the plain carelessness and disregard of children by other parents. Probably every parent is capable under certain circumstances of hurting his child, although almost always inadvertently. But then again, the parents who overtly abuse their children do not usually intend consciously to hurt them. Usually they are decent people.

SUICIDE

The most common psychiatric emergency, and most severe, is represented by the suicidal patient. It seems strange that life, which is precious to most people, should ever be abandoned willfully, yet people do kill themselves, many people. Exactly how many people is not certain. In this country alone over twenty thousand such deaths are reported each year, placing suicide among the top ten causes of death. Even according to this figure, suicide is a major public-health hazard—but the true frequency is much higher, probably by a factor of two or three. For religious and legal reasons, and also for psychological reasons, people prefer not to take formal notice of suicide. And so almost all drownings are counted as accidental; if someone falls off a building or wrecks his car, his death too will be regarded probably as an accident. A physician who takes an overdose of medicine may be recorded as killing himself inadvertently, as may an experienced hunter who shoots himself to death in the act of cleaning his gun.

There are other suicide statistics that may be relied on more confidently, but their meaning is unclear. It is known, for instance, that three times as many women try to kill themselves as men; yet three times as many men succeed as women. The difference has been explained sometimes by the fact that men are more likely to shoot themselves, while women are more inclined to take an overdose of pills, a method that leaves more room for error, perhaps, and is inherently less lethal. But why then would not women who are serious about committing suicide also shoot themselves? They have as ready access to firearms as men. Besides, pills are quite deadly enough when taken in sufficient number and under the proper circumstances. There are other facts about suicide that are just as hard to understand. Why do white men kill themselves more often than black men? Why does the number of suicides go down during time of war? Why does the rate of suicide go up with age? Why are the rates of suicide substantially different in different countries? For that matter why do psychiatrists as a group kill themselves proportionately more often than any other kind of physician and six times as often as pediatricians? Psychiatrists naturally take a lively interest in such questions, but even with a personal stake to focus their attention, they have been unable to answer them satisfactorily.

The Causes of Suicide

Suicide can have no single, cogent explanation because it is not the product of a single set of circumstances. Most people who kill themselves are in a state of depression, which itself has many different causes; but such an act may also grow out of a paranoid psychosis or a confusional state or some other condition. Indeed someone who tries to kill himself may not show any other evidence of mental illness at all. He may be trying to escape from an intolerable situation, such as the severe pain of a terminal illness, although even such apparently logical suicides have a strongly irrational component. There is always an emotional significance to the act of suicide. Every person who tries to kill himself has a daydream about death and dying in which the meaning of his act is hidden.

A young girl who has just had an argument with her father feels an overwhelming anger at herself, and disgust. With the thought of suicide in her mind, she cuts her arms with a dirty razor blade. Immediately she experiences a sense of relief, almost exhilaration, as if her intention was not to kill herself but to hurt or punish herself.

A woman in her forties hangs herself in the same hotel room in which her mother hanged herself twenty-five years previously. She leaves a note saying that she is going to join her mother. Death does not mean to her an ending of life, but a new beginning, a reunion, a rebirth.

A man who has been sentenced to hang poisons himself the day before his execution, not because he has grown tired of life one day early, but as an act of defiance. For that moment he is no longer subject to someone else's authority or wishes. For just that moment, he is no longer helpless, but has the power of life and death.

A woman slashes her wrist. After watching herself bleed for a while, she goes to the emergency room of a nearby hospital where her wrist is sutured. In subsequent months she does the same thing twice again. Each time she waits longer before going for help. And yet each time she tells the doctor that she is afraid of dying. She practices suicide, ironically, for just that reason. Her survival each time means to her that death cannot claim her, and so she is reassured. Another man has the same fear and accomplishes the same purpose by driving repeatedly when he is drunk. Both of them miscalculate finally, inevitably, and they kill themselves.

A sniper perched on top of a building shoots all day at passersby and in the evening shoots himself. He has left behind a notebook expressing hatred for everyone. The walls of his room are found to be covered with violent slogans, and he has written a letter to a friend calling for the killing of the President. Nowhere has he spoken of killing himself. Rather than setting out to commit suicide, he seems only to have caught himself in the line of fire of his own murderous rage, directed really at other people and at the world in general. Many people kill themselves when it is really someone else they want to kill.

A suicidal person may want to kill himself without necessarily wanting to be dead. For many it is the act itself that has meaning, a crying out or a giving up. A suicide may be a revenge upon someone who is loved or hated, or it may be an act of atonement or simply an expression of self-loathing. If these passions are communicated partially by an unsuccessful suicide attempt, the impetus to a further act of self-destruction diminishes, at least temporarily. For this reason it is somewhat unusual for a person to kill himself immediately after a previous suicide attempt.

Among those who appear to be suicidal are some who have no intention of killing themselves. They want to be rescued.

A psychiatry resident was called to his hospital admitting room to make an emergency evaluation. When he arrived, he saw a young woman, evidently his patient, moaning and crying very loudly. She sat by herself. A haggard man, who was apparently her husband, sat at the other end of a bench away from her, his head in his hands. The nurse on duty was even farther away: she sat in a glass cubicle staring angrily out at the woman, who by now seemed to be crying just as hard as she could. The patient calmed down immediately, however, when she and the resident were alone, and she gave the following history:

Her husband, she said, was only interested in pleasing himself. He never wanted to do what she wanted to do. She wanted to go to the movies that afternoon and he refused. She was fed up, and so, during lunch, right in front of him, she swallowed fifteen aspirin tablets. When asked by the resident why she took only fifteen from a bottle that held 250, she replied that she thought fifteen tablets were enough to kill herself. She was prepared to be admitted into a psychiatric hospital, she said, in order to teach her husband a lesson.

This woman did not really intend to kill herself. She wanted only to intimidate her husband. The pretense of suicide used in this way as a device to manipulate other people is called a *suicide gesture*. Suicide attempts that fail are very common, probably ten times as common as those that succeed; much is made, therefore, of distinguishing a serious suicide attempt from a gesture, which presumably is less dangerous, for it is less likely to be followed by a second fatal attempt. This woman was a typical example of the sort of person usually described as making a suicide gesture. She was immature, impulsive, histrionic, angry, depressed somewhat—although not very much—and, of course, manipulative, which is in sum an unprepossessing portrait of a human being.

Such a difficult person becomes a difficult patient to manage. She cannot be allowed to use the threat of suicide to get her way, for then she will try it again and again and very possibly kill herself inadvertently; on the other hand she must not simply be ignored. Like any other symptom such behavior is a sign of distress. A suicide gesture, in particular, however noisy and petulant, is a gesture of helplessness, and so a caring person should take any such act, however transparent, very seriously. There is in every gesture the thought of death, as there is, for that matter, in almost every earnest suicide attempt some last hope of surviving. No one is ever single-minded about wanting to die.

Suicide Prevention

The thought of suicide occurs usually in a person who is suffering an emotional illness, and is invariably only one manifestation of problems that exist in many areas of his life; but naturally the single, paramount consideration in taking care of any such person is to prevent him from killing himself. Suicide prevention has grown up, therefore, as a discipline unto itself. Various communities have organized suicide-prevention centers. Their most visible therapeutic activity is the operation of a "hot line," which is a telephone manned by interested but largely untrained individuals. They listen to anyone who calls on the telephone with the intention of notifying someone that he is going to kill himself. Anyone who does telephone is surely in need of help and worth listening to, but it may be surmised that those who are most actively suicidal do not call. In any case there are difficulties in managing a patient at the other end of a telephone line.

A lady called a municipal hospital to complain about a hospital bill, and because her complaints were excessive, perhaps, she was connected with the psychiatry resident on duty. She spoke to him willingly about her problems, which were many, and she mentioned in passing that she had just swallowed all the pills that she could find, including twenty barbiturates, and had had eight or ten glasses of Scotch besides.

Twenty barbiturates is potentially a lethal dose of medicine, especially in the presence of other drugs and large amounts of alcohol, so the resident was naturally concerned. He told her that he wanted to talk to her in person and that she should come to the hospital at once. She replied that she was fed up with psychiatrists and that she wasn't going anywhere. The resident offered then to send an ambulance to her home, but she refused to give her address—and there the matter rested throughout the next ten minutes of conversation.

The resident, who was young and not easily discouraged, decided to enlist the aid of the police. Steadfastly, he kept the woman on the telephone while they attempted to trace the call. He listened to her patiently, although she was angry and abusive. However, as time wore on, her speech became slurred, and he became increasingly worried that the police might not arrive in time to save her. Finally after two and one half hours of seemingly endless discussion characterized on his part by expressions of sympathy and interest and on hers by random vituperation, the police notified him that they had traced the wrong telephone number. It was then two o'clock in the morning.

The woman meanwhile had taken a few more pills and a few more shots of whiskey, and there seemed just as much reason to be worried about her then as ever. So for another two and one half hours the resident talked to her while the police once again attempted to trace the call. At four thirty in the morning the resident heard through the telephone a loud knock on the door of the woman's apartment, and she immediately hung up. He waited during the next hour for the patient to be brought to the hospital. When she was not, he called the police and was dismayed to find out that they had not entered her apartment because she had refused to open the door, and they were unwilling to proceed further without a warrant!

After ranting for a few minutes himself and promising to swear out a medical complaint against the woman, the resident managed to convince the police of the truly life-and-death character of the emergency. Reluctantly they agreed to return to her apartment. However, after twenty-four additional hours, the patient had not yet arrived at the hospital. Despite persistent inquiry, the resident could not find out from the police what had happened. In fact he could not locate any of the policemen he had spoken to during the night, nor was there any record of their conversation.

The influence a therapist has with a patient comes entirely from their relationship, which cannot grow up casually during a telephone conversation. Still, the prospect of suicide is so awful that even such a fragile connection, if that is all there is between them, must not be broken. The therapist is not entitled to hang up. In dealing with a disagreeable patient he may not shrug hopelessly or become exasperated. This particular patient may have survived, after all, because that resident was willing to endure such an inconvenient and, as it turned out, inconclusive conversation. Even if he accomplished nothing else, he may have distracted her from taking enough pills to kill herself, although he would never know for sure. Psychiatrists and psychologists have to become accustomed to uncertain endings. They only know their patients for a little while, and the final results of their efforts are not usually known to them—unless by some misfortune a patient dies or kills himself while still under their care.

Other general measures have been suggested as a means of lowering the suicide rate. These include more religious training, closer-knit families, less pressure at school, more meaningful work, more research into and education of the public to the problem of suicide, and so on. Similar programs of mental hygiene have also been recommended for the prevention of alcoholism, drug abuse, and mental illness in general—and venereal diseases, for that matter, and all sorts of other diseases, and for crime; and probably these programs would be helpful if they could be implemented. But social institutions change very slowly, and no such program is likely to be applied systematically. Consequently the prevention of suicide comes down to the prevention of particular suicides.

The Management of the Suicidal Patient

The suicidal patient comes to the attention of his family or physician either because he has in some way expressed thoughts of killing himself or because he has already made an unsuccessful attempt. Less commonly a patient appears in such a depressed state of mind that his potential for suicide is obvious. It must be obvious, indeed, before his family or friends will take note of it, for the thought of suicide is too frightening for them to consider readily. Sometimes they will disregard the most explicit evidence. This blindness to the feelings of the depressed person often seems to him to be disinterest; in reaction to it, he may become more depressed and more acutely suicidal. The following case history is an example.

A thirty-seven-year-old woman, who had been married for only three years and was childless, left the immediate neighborhood of her parents for the first time in her life to join her husband, who was an officer in the air force, recently assigned to a base in England. At first she looked forward to this adventure but within a few weeks of her arrival seemed upset. She found that she had trouble making friends. She spent much of her time alone in her apartment, moving furniture back and forth, always unsatisfied with its appearance. Money problems preoccupied her, seemingly out of proportion to their real financial circumstances. She claimed they couldn't afford to live. As time went on, she developed a variety of physical symptoms, including loss of appetite and nausea, and she had trouble sleeping. She began to have trouble getting along with her husband. She complained bitterly of his lack of attention to her. No one needed her or wanted her, she said. Her life served no purpose. He assured her that he did care for her, and to prove it made arrangements to take her on vacation. For just a while she seemed to feel better, but for only a little while. Soon after setting off on the trip, she lost interest in traveling and became apathetic in general, remaining in her hotel room and crying much of the time. She engaged in repetitive conversations with her husband about the provisions of her will. Finally one night she went to sleep early. When her husband tried unsuccessfully to rouse her an hour later, he realized she had taken an overdose of sleeping pills. It came as a surprise to him. Only then did he call a psychiatrist.

* * *

This husband demonstrated a fixed ignorance of his wife's condition. Despite abundant evidence of her depression, and reason also to think she was preoccupied by thoughts of her own death, he never once considered the possibility of her killing herself. Yet he loved her. Perhaps it was because he loved her that suicide was unthinkable; but by looking away from her, he gave her permission to die. With great regularity suicidal patients announce in some way their intention to kill themselves, and, regularly, that announcement is ignored. In such a way they are confirmed in their decision, and families and other people are made into accomplices.

Determining the Risk of Suicide

In order to prevent a suicide it is necessary first to suspect that it may happen. The fact is that anyone who is significantly depressed is likely to think of killing himself and may under certain circumstances undertake to do so. Most, luckily, do not. An important indication of suicide risk is the level of hopelessness. Any feeling, any situation, can be tolerated if it is seen to be temporary. If the depressed person sees no way out of his problems, the risk to his life is considerable. However, if he has despaired, he will usually indicate so to anyone who bothers to ask. No one should hesitate to ask. If the thought of suicide has not occurred to the depressed person, he will not seize upon the idea simply because it had been mentioned to him.

Other factors that should be kept in mind include these:

A prior history of a suicide attempt. More than half of all successful suicides have made such an attempt. Each succeeding attempt is likely to be more serious, providing less warning and leaving less room for rescue. If any systematic program is developed to prevent suicide, it should be directed at the large number of people who have survived such an attempt, for they are the population at risk.

The extent of planning for death. Many people who have decided to kill themselves make plans for the disposition of their property or their remains. They may want to arrange for the care of their survivors. These final plans are often made openly, as are the plans they make for the act of suicide itself. As the suicidal person comes closer to killing himself, his intentions become more specific. Anyone who talks even vaguely of killing himself must be attended to, but someone who says that he has eighty-seven pills in his medicine cabinet which he intends to swallow next Thursday when no one is at home must be taken very seriously indeed.

The existence of family. Suicide is a complication of loneliness and occurs frequently, for example, among the recently widowed and the divorced. Someone living alone is especially at risk. The individual's past life is also relevant. The loss of a parent at an early age is a frequent finding in the lives of people who kill themselves. The correlation is even more striking when the death of the parent was the result of suicide. Suicide is contagious. When a famous person is reported in a newspaper as having killed himself, a wave of suicide follows.

The presence of a precipitating event, usually a loss, which may be physical. A hysterectomy may provoke suicide, as does breast surgery, probably because of the special psychological meaning these parts of the body have for women. Mutilative surgery of any kind may be followed by a depression. Also a chronic disease of any kind, if it is sufficiently painful or incapacitating, may result in suicide.

The excessive use of alcohol, or other drugs. These intoxicating substances are associated with a high rate of suicide, in part because they cause depression, and in part because they are used by persons who are already depressed. Barbiturates and other sleeping medications are dangerous and particularly subject to abuse.

*   *   *

An unsure indicator of the risk of suicide is the patient's clinical course. Someone who is depressed may look and feel better, not because his condition is resolved, but because he has resolved his conflict about killing himself. Deciding once and for all to end everything brings a sense of relief. It is the small measure of calm that people have when they know they need not struggle any longer, when all of their ambitions, anxieties, and responsibilities are behind them. Another uncertain indicator of the danger of suicide is the patient's stated intent. Someone may deny suicidal thoughts in order to deceive. So, while an admission of the wish to kill oneself may be relied on, a denial cannot.

Anyone is liable to kill himself, just as anyone is vulnerable to illness or accident or to any of the other sudden calamities of life. Suicide is only one kind of weakness inherent in the human condition, but some people are more in danger of it than others. They are those who are impulsive or isolated or especially dependent, or those who feel especially guilty or resentful. And there are those who simply have too few emotional resources to cope with any special stress in their lives. Treatment of these individuals, therefore, is directed at their particular weaknesses and incapacities.

The Supportive Therapy of Suicidal Patients

Anyone who mentions the possibility of killing himself must be taken seriously; if he makes an unsuccessful attempt on his own life, however insincere and inconsequential it may seem to be, he must be regarded as seriously disturbed. Such a person should be referred to a psychiatrist or a psychologist for evaluation and treatment. But proper treatment goes beyond what a professional can offer during the one or two hours a week the patient spends in his office. The patient should be observed closely and continually so that a serious attempt at suicide can be anticipated and prevented, perhaps by hospitalization. The seriousness of his intent to injure himself is likely to change suddenly, in response to events or to sudden changes of mood. Evidence of a worsening depression includes the tendency to withdraw from friends and family. The usual pursuits of the patient may no longer appeal to him. His work may suffer and he may lose interest in sex. The so-called vegetative signs of depression—retardation of physical activity, loss of appetite, and insomnia—may become more severe. If the patient is known to have a specific underlying illness, such as a manic-depressive psychosis, he must be observed for a return of those symptoms that he has had in the past. When patients fall ill from relapsing disorders, often they develop the same premonitory symptoms in the beginning of each recurrence, which if recognized early allows an early start to treatment. The medications used for treating depression, for instance, usually take two to three weeks to work and should be given as soon as possible to diminish the risk of suicide during this dangerous period.

Naturally the patient should not be allowed to have weapons. Guns in particular should be taken away. He should not have in his possession a potentially lethal dose of medicine. Physicians often prescribe drugs with abandon, especially sleeping medicines. All medicines should be held for the patient and doled out, even if doing so is perceived as insulting.

But the helping person can do more. He can help the patient find an alternative to dying. The reality of life is scarcely ever as hopeless as a depressed person imagines it to be. Those acting as therapist should listen to the patient's worries and consider with him possible solutions to his problems, not because those suggestions will necessarily seem feasible just then, but because offering them is an expression of concern, and is comforting. As withdrawn as the suicidal patient may seem to be, he will respond to a friendly person. It is possible to help even those who seem to want no help.

Of course not everyone is willing to extend himself in the aid of such a patient.

A woman at the age of nineteen already had a long psychiatric history, including a hospitalization following a suicide attempt when she was fifteen. Although she had had years of therapy, she had still a great number of emotional problems that intruded into every area of her life and made her miserable. She was overly dependent on her parents to assist her through the ordinary business of the day. Her mother laid out her clothes for her in the morning, and her father packed her lunch and cleaned her room. She insisted that they listen to her whenever she wanted to talk, and with that in mind, she once burst into their bedroom when they were in the midst of sexual intercourse. At the same time, she was usually angry at them. She ridiculed them for being ignorant and clumsy. She had similar ambivalent relationships with everyone. She was punished continually in school for talking in class and on one occasion for throwing a sandwich at her teacher. She had been fired from two jobs. Her style with people was clinging and demanding and insulting, all at once, an unworkable design for getting along. In addition she was obese, had pustular acne and a lisp. She had never dated a boy. Because she was alone almost always, she felt rejected and depressed and would take to her room for weeks at a time. She was terribly unhappy.

Her relationship with her therapist was marked on her part by those same perversities that affected her relationships with everyone and that made her unloved and unlovable. She scolded and derided him for his shortcomings, which she was able to describe accurately and in detail. She demanded appointments in the middle of the night. Once when he was out, she ate everything in his office refrigerator. She also saw to it that his bill was never paid on time.

One evening she followed him home from his office and rang his doorbell. When he came to the door, right before his eyes, she swallowed seventy-five sleeping capsules, after which she announced that she wanted to come in and lie down. He replied to her in a rage that he would not allow her to manipulate him any further, and he slammed the door shut. She went out to her car, which she had parked in his driveway, and remained there all night. Perhaps she expected him to come out to her after all and rescue her. Perhaps she did not intend, really, to die, but it made no difference in the end. In the morning she was found dead.

What excuse can there be for that psychiatrist? However difficult his patient was, he should have saved her. Whatever theoretical or personal reason he gave himself for not going out to her or for not calling the police, he was wrong. She was entitled to live. There are some people like this psychiatrist, who are defective somehow as people, however well trained they may be and however elevated their professional status. They have lost the ordinary human qualities of sympathy and common sense. This girl needed someone to be firm with her, perhaps, but not rejecting. She needed someone to be patient with her too. A therapist may not allow his common decency to be worn away by the exasperating and provocative behavior of any patient.

An enthusiastic, resolute person who cares for a patient and does not readily despair offers that relationship that is the foundation for psychotherapy and that is no less valuable for being provided, as it may be and often is, by someone who is relatively untrained.

Hospitalization *
If it is plain that a person is going to kill himself, he should be admitted into a hospital, even against his wishes. Transporting the individual from the community at large into

---

* For a comparison of outpatient treatment and in-hospital treatment, see pp. 49–54.

an institution can only be a partial and temporary response to his problems. The mere fact that he is put away does not turn his life into happier channels. His distress has not been disposed of—nor have the causes of it. But hospitalization, conceived of as one piece of a therapeutic regimen, accomplishes a number of purposes:

1. A clear demonstration is made to the patient of a willingness to take his problem seriously. His fate is made to seem important. Someone does care. Hospitalization is a formal and signal recognition of the fact that the patient is in crisis and vulnerable as a result. Sometimes his family only then becomes fully aware of that fact. Having seized their attention, the therapist has an opportunity to influence the manner in which they all relate to each other, for the turbulence of a crisis within the family allows all of its members to step out of their accustomed roles and be different.

2. The patient is separated, it is hoped, from those tools that he might use to commit suicide. It is presumed that in this protected environment he will be unable to shoot himself or accumulate enough medicine to kill himself. Also an alert staff can observe him more constantly and carefully than can be accomplished by his family when he is at home.

3. The environment of the hospital, if it is a good hospital, surrounds the patient in a therapeutic milieu. The patient is brought out of isolation into contact with people who are understanding. He may learn to see himself through their eyes and become more accepting of himself. There is time to explore his thoughts and feelings and the sum of the circumstances of his life that have brought him to the brink of suicide.

Unfortunately mental hospitals are not well run very often, and hospitalization does not always achieve its goals. Moreover the entire process of hospitalization is not always entered into in good faith. The physician and the patient's family sometimes use the hospital, unconsciously perhaps, as a device for discharging their responsibility. Once the patient is out of sight, they tell themselves they have done everything they could for him. They step back and allow his destiny to unwind by itself. From that time on no one seems to be in direct charge of the patient, and if he kills himself at some subsequent point, no one is accountable. The hospital is treated as an alternative to treatment rather than as part of treatment.

It may be deemed prudent to hospitalize a patient unnecessarily rather than risk a suicide, but being in a hospital can work to the patient's disadvantage. Life within is gloomy, uncomfortable, and sometimes threatening, and characterized above all by an implacable and devastating boredom, with nowhere to go and nothing to do. Because the patient is separated from his family and from everyone else of importance in his life, he may become more rather than less isolated. His family may adjust to being without him, so that even when he leaves the hospital, he comes home only as an uneasy visitor. If he has been away long enough, he may have lost his job. Real treatment usually begins not when a patient enters the hospital, but when he leaves it.

Most disconcerting of all is the fact that bringing a suicidal patient into the hospital does not necessarily guarantee his safety.

A twenty-year-old corporal was brought to an army station hospital in Europe. When examined he gave an account of being singled out by God. God had spoken to him that very day and commanded him to obey his instructions, or the sun would grow cold in the sky, the stars would fall, and the earth would shiver into pieces. His first instruction was to destroy the television set at the Officers' Club, which he did, and to throw away all of his clothes and walk naked in God's sight through the streets, which he did also. He spoke of these things readily, although he seemed abstracted throughout the interview. Also he laughed strangely from time to time.

The psychiatrist who examined him recognized his state of beatitude as one expression of a paranoid schizophrenia. Because such an illness has a potential for violent behavior, the patient was asked especially if he had been instructed by God to injure anyone or kill himself. He replied that he had not, and he lapsed into silence.

That particular hospital had no psychiatric ward, so arrangements were made to have the patient evacuated by helicopter to a larger facility. In the meantime a medical corpsman was instructed to observe the patient constantly. He did just that. The disturbed young man lay apparently asleep on a stretcher, while the corpsman stood alongside and looked at him. Suddenly the patient sat up, swung one foot off the stretcher and onto a windowsill. He then crashed through the window, which was closed, and fell three stories to his death.

Perhaps had the patient been tied to the stretcher, he would not have found it so easy to contrive his death. But there was no special reason to think he was considering suicide; besides, it is not possible to keep people tied up in a bundle for any length of time, whatever the danger. One might argue that had he been on a psychiatric ward, the windows would have been screened, and he would have been safe. But that same week, at the hospital where he was waiting to be taken, a patient on the psychiatric ward committed suicide by stuffing toilet paper down his throat, and a second patient walked off the ward and up to the roof and jumped off from there. The fact is that suicide occurs with some regularity in psychiatric hospitals. If someone is determined to kill himself, he will find the opportunity wherever he happens to be.

There is a real issue, then, that must be joined in the evaluation of a suicidal patient: does the risk to his life justify the disruption of his life caused by hospitalization? Do the benefits of a particular hospital outweigh the benefits of remaining at home? It is not a matter that can be decided one way all the time as a matter of principle. The "safe" solution over the short run may not be wise, or even safe.

After an Unsuccessful Suicide Attempt
The weeks that follow an unsuccessful suicide attempt are particularly trying to the patient and his family. Those expressions of concern that welled up spontaneously from everyone in the immediate aftermath of the suicide act have by then subsided. Left remaining is only the usual and accustomed routine of life. No one behaves any differently than he ever did. Invariably, the patient feels discouraged—disappointed a little because the world has not changed after all, and disappointed a little because he is still alive. To fail at the essentially simple task of suicide is to pile an ignominious failure onto a life that is felt already to be a failure. Because he is not actually dead, his family is disbelieving of his intention to kill himself. They settle into a wary and uncomfortable silence which further isolates the patient. In this atmosphere a second suicide attempt becomes possible and probably easier than the first. The seriousness of a first suicide attempt is not an infallible guide to the likelihood of a second.

A thirty-five-year-old woman, a lawyer, was despondent over the dissolution of her third marriage. One morning she sat over breakfast, wondering whether she should go to work that day or stay at home and kill herself. She decided finally that she had no good reason to live. She swallowed a hundred sleeping tablets, made a careful incision into an artery in her wrist, and put her head into the oven after turning on the gas. Luckily a few minutes later the oven exploded, setting fire to the kitchen. The fireman who arrived on the scene brought the woman to a hospital, where her life was saved. Except for second-degree burns around the face, which took a few months to heal, she did very well thereafter. This deadly serious try at suicide was never followed by another. She entered psychotherapy and a year later made a fourth, this time apparently happy, marriage.

Unfortunately, many more examples could be given of patients whose first attempts at suicide were half-hearted, but who killed themselves subsequently nevertheless.

During the critical period that follows an attempt at suicide, the therapist must see his patient frequently and be available to him constantly, at least by telephone. A second try at suicide, if it is allowed to happen, is likely to be more determined than the first. Besides, luck sometimes runs the other way, and even a feeble attempt may succeed. The therapist must also be careful not to respond to the patient's gloom by becoming gloomy himself, or angry or despairing. It is helpful if his own attitude toward life is optimistic, for to an extent his patient's point of view will reflect his own.

After a Successful Suicide

Whoever takes care of very disturbed, suicidal patients will one day have to confront the fact that a patient under his care has killed himself. Naturally it is no wonder if someone with a severe mental illness should die of it; but still the therapist wonders always if he misunderstood his patient somehow, or said the wrong thing or did the wrong thing. He wonders if he was responsible for that person's death.

A fifty-five-year-old woman came to the doors of a state hospital, saying that she had come to spend the rest of her life. She gave only a brief account of herself, saying that her life had been uninteresting and uneventful. She was an only child of divorced parents. She was close to her mother and had always shared an apartment with her until her mother died of cancer six months previously. Her father owned a home only fifty miles away, but she had never been invited to visit him. She had not seen him in ten years, and they spoke by telephone only once or twice a year. No one else in the world mattered to her. She had never married. She had few friends, none of whom she had bothered to see for years. Although she was a bookkeeper, she had not worked for years because of persistent abdominal cramps. She had recently undergone an operation for this problem and was told afterward that she too had cancer. The thought of being so sick didn't bother her, though. She continued to have pain, but her only real distress came from thinking about her dead mother. She could not live alone, she said, and so she came to the hospital because there was no place else to go. If she was not admitted, she went on, she would kill herself. She was not psychotic and, despite the gloomy narrative she told, she did not seem very depressed. A state hospital is not a good place to go for someone who has no place to go; but nevertheless, she was admitted, not only because of her threat of suicide, but because she obviously needed some sort of help.

She settled at once into the dreary and half-alive routine of a state hospital. Soon she showed no evidence of mental illness at all, other than the underlying defects of personality that had allowed her to lead such a narrow and inhibited life for so many years. She communicated freely with staff and developed a friendly, even warm, relationship with her psychiatrist. Using that relationship as a lever, the psychiatrist began to explore the possibility of constructing a meaningful life for the patient outside the hospital. With the patient pulling quite firmly in the other direction, arrangements were made for her to take an apartment nearby the hospital. She was helped to get a part-time job, and her friends were instructed that she was returning to the community and was in need of their interest and attention. These various efforts were drawn together, and on the appointed day, the patient left the hospital.

She survived for a time. She cooperated with the efforts that the hospital staff made to help her. She worked and saw people, but there was no joy for her in living. Finally, abruptly, she left her apartment to go live with her father, although she was still uninvited and, it turned out, unwanted. Only a few days later she returned again to the state hospital with two pieces of luggage and her important belongings. Although she once again threatened suicide, her psychiatrist refused to permit her readmission. He promised to see her on the outside and help her, but he was worried, he told her, about her disappearing forever into the hospital. He sent her home with two attendants. They unpacked for her and returned the next morning to do her shopping. She gave them a list of groceries she said she needed, but when they came back from the store, they discovered her in the bathroom. She had slashed her wrists. She was dead. She had left behind a note which read:

> *Give the groceries to Mrs. Smith. See Mr. James about will. Don't call my father. He doesn't give a damn. I'm too much trouble for everyone. I don't need to live anymore. Good-bye.*

Conceivably this women might not have committed suicide had she been readmitted to the hospital. But the psychiatrist could not know that ahead of time. He knew when he turned her away that she might kill herself, and so, in a way, he was gambling with her life; but any other decision would have been a gamble also. He thought readmission would encourage her to settle permanently for the compromised and unsatisfactory existence of a patient in a state hospital. And might she not then have become more isolated and vulnerable? Sooner or later she would have to be discharged, and how well would she manage then? Every treatment has varied and unpredictable results. Those who care for the mentally ill, or for anyone who is ill, have to learn to live with their mistakes, for they make them inevitably. All they may be certain of, and should be certain of, is that their decision is careful, informed, and compassionate. There is no time for regrets; for even after a patient has killed himself, even then there is still something left to do. The therapist has to help the family, as much as he can, to confront and overcome the same frustration and guilt and emptiness that he himself feels.

There is a last consideration—or perhaps it is the first: Is someone entitled to kill himself? Suicide is not a private act, of course. It is a reproach against everyone, an abandonment that leaves everyone bereft. Children, naturally, suffer especially. Perhaps the person who sets out to commit suicide cannot help himself, but he should understand that he is committing an act that is harmful to others. Sometimes that thought is enough to deter him. But what of the patient, such as the woman above, who has no family to survive her? Should she be permitted to take her own life?

The fact is that most patients who are suicidal when they are in the throes of a depression may very well want to live when they feel better, which may be only a few weeks later. How tragic it would be for them to have died during that transitory moment in their lives when their judgment was clouded. And there are people who make an attempt on their lives at a time when they experience a disappointment—an unrequited love, perhaps—which only a year later, if they have survived, seems inconsequential to them. But still, there are those who seem stubbornly intent on killing themselves. They are saved time and time again until, finally, they evade their rescuers and die. As they make ready to exit from life, they may leave behind a message, just as this woman did, indicating their determination to die. These notes are terrible to read. Their authors seem to stand beside the pages, barely out of reach, forlorn, angry, embittered—yet, in that last letter, still trying to influence the world in some way one last time, still trying to communicate something. Then they turn away. They declare the world not fit for them. Finding life not worth living, should they be allowed to die?

A young physician beginning his internship came to wonder about the meaning of life. He was stimulated to these musings by an extraordinary patient who came in one day for treatment. The man was elderly, and to a great extent incapacitated. One arm was evidently paralyzed. With his other arm he propelled himself along on a little cart, for he was missing both legs. It was apparent from the glasses that he wore that his vision was poor, and he was partially deaf. The diseases he suffered from included diabetes, peripheral and cerebral vascular disease, and heart disease. He had had many other transient conditions, including urinary and lung infections. He had lost most of his teeth. He had an ugly, scaly rash which covered his chest and which, as it happened, was the reason he came to the clinic that day.

The doctor prescribed an ointment for the man's rash, then drew him aside. He sat with him and then, after a moment's hesitation, asked him directly how he found it possible to live with all of his illnesses. He wanted to know if this man, who was so miserably afflicted, found purpose in his life.

The man replied that he was not a religious person, so he had not stopped to wonder about life. "But things aren't too bad," he went on. "I sit around and watch TV, which I can see a little if I get up close. Or I visit my daughter in her apartment downstairs. She has a little kid, and we play ball together on the carpet. Or I tell her stories. I like going outside, and the park isn't very far away, you know. And besides, I can still play checkers. I win. They call me the one-armed bandit," he said with a laugh.

*   *   *

It would not be exactly right to describe this man as stoical or courageous. The fact is, he simply enjoyed life. He was cheerful.

Whether or not someone is happy or miserable has surprisingly little to do with the circumstances of his life, but is a matter of perspective only—a perspective that changes over time, for many reasons. A suicidal patient, therefore, who despairs does not despair of the real world but only of a particular and personal view of it. He may be able to describe the emptiness of his life so poignantly and vividly that he convinces everyone that, indeed, there is no alternative to dying, but no one's life is necessarily miserable. His distress is not inherent in the world, not even in *his* world, but rather in the way he conceives it. Someone who has a clearer vision of the world should be able to convince him to live—and often does, with patience and the passage of time.

4 PSYCHOSIS

PSYCHOSES are mental disorders of such severity that they affect the whole of an individual's personality and interfere with his understanding of the world to the degree that he is said to be divorced from reality. Of course, no one is in perfect touch with reality. Everyone organizes his current experience of the world in terms of his previous experience. In that sense everyone is prejudiced. Everyone lives in his own world. Nevertheless it seems reasonable to distinguish a special group of disorders characterized by disturbances of feeling, thought, and perception so severe that they serve to isolate anyone so affected from everyone else. That person then behaves in a fashion judged by ordinary people to be grossly abnormal. And at the same time, he suffers greatly. These disorders are called the psychoses.

Psychotic states can develop from physical diseases of almost any type. A person may become psychotic, for instance, from a head injury, stroke, heart attack, infection, or from any illness that produces a toxic condition. There are psychoses that result from tumors and from vitamin deficiencies or metabolic diseases. Drugs of abuse, which sometimes stimulate the rarefied and congenial sense of being high, some other times produce the distress of a frank psychosis. The management of all these psychoses is largely the management of the underlying condition that produces them.

There is another group of psychoses of more obscure etiology, the so-called functional psychoses. They include, first, the schizophrenias in their various forms, and, second, the affective psychoses, the latter being conditions that make themselves most evident by alterations of affect or mood. These headings do not refer to two distinct illnesses or even families of illness; they are descriptive terms only. Over the years they have been defined and redefined. Schizophrenia, before it was called schizophrenia, was once thought of as a dementia, a mental deterioration like senility. Then it was discovered—or decided, at least—that schizophrenia more closely resembled other conditions characterized in part by severe disturbances of behavior. In fact these various conditions were judged to be merely different forms of the same illness. And other related forms were described. The condition was redefined and renamed. Then a number of illnesses previously indistinguishable from these others were found to derive from special causes such as infections or metabolic defects, and so they were dropped from the concept of schizophrenia. As time wore on, new conditions have been added and others subtracted. There is a syndrome called pseudo-neurotic schizophrenia, which, as might be guessed readily, is supposed to be a form of schizophrenia that resembles neurosis. A related disorder is manifested by the borderline patient. "Borderline what?" one may ask; but the fact is that "borderline" is discussed usually as a state in itself, of no precise character and no definite boundaries, but in the general neighborhood of psychosis and schizophrenia. Some people speak of a borderline border line. Such is the current state of psychiatric nomenclature.

Our appreciation of the affective psychoses has undergone a similar evolution. Our names for them have changed, and more important, so has our understanding of them as diseases. One example is the manic-depressive psychosis. Current work on the genetic transmission of this illness has tended to show that it is in reality a number of illnesses that have different prognoses and different treatments.

Therapists are susceptible to "fashion" in the diagnosis of mental illness, so that the prevalence of a particular condition varies from place to place and time to time. Given a certain type of patient, the English are inclined to pronounce him manic-depressive, while the Americans are more likely to call him schizophrenic. Some clinicians with the usual penchant of psychiatrists for finding in-between conditions may describe him as schizo-affective, which is a little of one and a little of the other. The advent of new drugs always encourages the diagnosis of the illness for which that drug is effective. When phenothiazines became available and were found to help schizophrenia, there was a prejudice on the part of doctors to find that anyone who was psychotic was suffering from schizophrenia, more or less. There were correspondingly fewer and fewer manic-depressives. More recently, when an effective agent for the treatment of manic-depressive illness was also discovered, the reported prevalence of that disease began to rise again. Few cases of either psychotic state are so unequivocal that a group of psychiatrists is likely to agree entirely upon them.

However diffuse these clinical entities may be, however incomplete our knowledge of them, we must struggle with them nevertheless, for patients afflicted with such disorders occupy the greater number of our hospital beds and the greater portion of the time and attention of all those charged with the care of the mentally ill. They are, therefore, the central problem of modern psychiatry. They are grouped together in these chapters not only because historically they have been thought to be related in some way, but because they have in common the important tendency to relapse: acute episodes are likely to recur repeatedly over the course of a lifetime. Because each attack is extraordinarily disruptive, the fact that a person has such an illness may become the most important circumstance of his life. Nothing else matters to him so much, for however well he may seem to be at any given time, the possibility of a recurrence looms ominously before him. And yet there are few conditions in all of medicine that are so chronic and yet respond so well to treatment, especially to treatment administered during the crucial periods between acute episodes, when the patient is at home. The purpose of these chapters is to describe the principles of supportive psychotherapy as they apply to these most serious mental illnesses.

SCHIZOPHRENIA

There is a stereotype of a schizophrenic patient.

A young man who has always been somewhat withdrawn and unhappy worsens suddenly. He hears voices warning of a plot against him. Consequently, he hides in his room, refusing even to come out to wash, and refusing to eat because the food may be poisoned.

He is admitted involuntarily into a mental hospital, where he develops increasingly peculiar ideas, including the conviction that he has become pregnant. He engages in eccentric and sometimes unpleasant behavior, spitting at people who walk by. His mood shifts unpredictably from giddy laughter to sobbing. Sometimes he is violent, on one occasion coming up behind an attendant and striking him on the head with a shoe.

He recovers somewhat from this acute psychotic episode,

but as the years go by he relapses over and over. Each hospitalization is longer than the one before, and between hospitalizations he had become increasingly strange, both in appearance and behavior. For example, he wears the same shirt every day for a month. He spends hours in the bathroom washing his hands and combing his hair. He withdraws from everyone, including his family, and may go days without speaking to another person. More time passes. His parents die one after the other, and he retires permanently into a state hospital. In this final stage of his life he no longer demonstrates extremes of mood or behavior. The way he is on any particular day is the way he is likely to be any other day. He sits by himself, frozen, in a corner of a room, facing the wall, shaking his legs rhythmically, sucking all of the fingers on one hand, soiling himself, lost in a mysterious and terrible reverie, forever.

This unfortunate man has a real existence; he lives in a back ward of a state mental hospital together with others who are similarly incapacitated. He lives also, perhaps more fully, in the mind of society, for his awful plight and the plight of other truly chronic schizophrenics has fixed itself in the imaginations not only of authors and artists of all sorts, but of public officials, lawyers and judges, even nurses and physicians, including some psychiatrists. His life has become a stereotype, even a caricature, of all schizophrenics, who are consequently regarded as if they were doomed to follow his inexorable course. This then is the image that haunts everyone who considers the schizophrenic: a chronic, hopeless patient who is unresponsive and incomprehensible, isolated, useless, dirty and disgusting, violent, and crazy.

Such a person is repulsive to us and so we conceive no plans for his treatment except to put him away from us in an institution. It is said that a chronic schizophrenic suffers from three conditions: his underlying illness, whatever that is; the effects of long-term drug administration, which are many and varied; and the effects of living great periods of his life in institutions. Perhaps there is a fourth: the attitude of society toward him. Without question these last two influences are the most debilitating and traumatic of all. Because of our preconceived idea of the schizophrenic, he is put away in institutions, and because he is put away in such places, he comes to resemble our preconceived idea of him. So the very act of identifying a person as schizophrenic becomes destructive. Because he is thought to be useless, he is not offered work. Because he is supposed to be violent, he is often locked up arbitrarily and without regard to his civil rights. Because he is supposed to be crazy, he is shunned, sometimes even by his family. Because he is considered to be unresponsive and intractable, he often goes untreated, seen by a psychiatrist intermittently and just long enough to prescribe medicine. The schizophrenic is hampered cruelly by these circumstances. And a dreadful irony makes this bad situation intolerable. The fact is that the clinical course of the particular patient described above is *not* typical of schizophrenia. Schizophrenics vary among themselves just as people do in general. No one can guess what will happen in the future to someone who has suffered a schizophrenic episode. He may do very well. And far from being intractable, schizophrenia is an illness that is especially amenable to treatment, although the elements of the treatment process are varied and must be drawn together into a rational scheme. Some of these elements are the benefits of work and close association with other people such as family and friends. They include, in short, just those emotional supports that are customarily denied to the schizophrenic because of society's stereotype of him. Psychotherapy is important: there is no mental illness that is affected so powerfully by it as schizophrenia. There is no patient who, left alone, is likely to follow such a malignant course, and yet with psychotherapy can do so well, as the schizophrenic.

Schizophrenia is not defined by its clinical course, which is variable, but by certain characteristic disturbances of thought and feeling, and of behavior. These disturbances also appear to an extent that varies from one person to another and varies also over time; so that when reference is made in these chapters to *the schizophrenic*, it should be understood that no single schizophrenic, let alone all of them, is being described rigorously. Nevertheless it is by these parameters that the diagnosis is made.

Thinking. The schizophrenic suffers a disorganization of thinking. During the acute psychotic reaction he may experience an uncontrollable rush of thought, one idea chasing after another or blocking another. Consequently his use of language as he communicates his thoughts is faulty, obscure to a listener, and sometimes incomprehensible. This loosening of associations may be caused by an anxious feeling or by the intrusion of an unwanted impulse. The process of thinking is so fragile that he may be disconcerted by a murmuring sound from the next apartment. At times he may become so distracted that he seems to be in a world of his own. Sometimes he makes up his own words, as if only a private language could describe that special world. At other times the defect in his thinking may disappear or be so subtle as to escape notice.

Feeling. Affect, which is a quality of emotional tone, some aspect of feeling, is disordered in the schizophrenic, so that he is impaired in his ability to react emotionally. Consequently feelings he demonstrates are likely to be inappropriate to the ideas he is expressing at the same time, or to the situation he is in. A person may laugh when speaking about the death of a parent, or cry while watching a baseball game. This discrepancy is a reflection partly of a discontinuity of thought. It is not the death of the parent but rather the memory of him that makes the schizophrenic laugh. But in addition there is probably a disturbance of affect primary to the schizophrenic process, for an affected person may experience sudden intense emotions, especially anxiety and rage. Sometimes the pull of his feelings is in opposite directions, immobilizing him. A second disturbance of feeling that appears in acute, but more commonly chronic, schizophrenics is a blunting of affect, an apathy. Events of great emotional significance elicit only a drab, unexcited response. Ordinary social intercourse, which generates all sorts of subtle and discrete emotional states in ordinary people, may leave the schizophrenic unaffected, unresponsive, and wooden.

Growing out of these primary disturbances of feeling and thought are a host of secondary symptoms, which may or may not appear, including delusions, hallucinations, and any of a wide range of eccentric and self-defeating behaviors, some of which are described in examples given throughout these chapters.

Investigators have attempted to explain the disturbances of thought and feeling as a function of a single, still more primitive, defect that could be regarded then as the true, underlying cause of schizophrenia. These theories are diverse. A brief sample: All of the intricate symptomatology of this illness has been attributed by some to the unconscious, but almost willful, tendency of the schizophrenic to isolate himself from everyone. His hallucinations, delusions, and infantile behavior are regarded simply as a consequence of that withdrawal. Others have explained these same phenomena on the basis of unusual, inborn sensitivities, or as the result of disturbances of communication which are learned in the midst of family life and fostered by the family. Another account explains schizophrenia as a disorder of perception. The schizophrenic cannot pay attention properly. He cannot distinguish what is relevant to a situation. He may not even be able to perceive himself properly, which is why he sometimes confuses his own feelings and impulses with those of other people.

The most commonly accepted theory explains schizophrenia, at least in some cases, as a genetically determined, inheritable, biochemical disorder of the brain, probably reflecting an enzymatic deficiency of some sort. But it seems that even when such a physical defect exists, the illness may not manifest itself. Somehow the environment in which the schizophrenic grows up is crucial to the development of the disease and its subsequent course. It is probable that an acute psychosis develops only when the individual undergoes stress. Stress in this sense need not be something dramatic, but rather is made up usually out of the intangible demands of everyday life—out of the need to grow up and leave behind the important people of childhood, or, perhaps, out of the demands of ordinary friendship and intimacy, or of adult sexuality. If the individual who is genetically predisposed to schizophrenia has developed a resilient and capable personality, he may never become sick, for he handles all of the difficult problems of life before they become stressful. Even if he has been sick once already, he may never relapse a second time if he can be helped to grow stronger and less vulnerable. Unfortunately the schizophrenic may respond to stress instead by fantasizing, withdrawing, constructing a delusional scheme, or by exhibiting any of the stereotyped and maladroit behaviors that in sum make up the ineffective, unworkable life of the chronic schizophrenic.

The therapy of the schizophrenic, then, is twofold:

1. To save him from repeated psychotic episodes by minimizing the stresses to which he is subject.

2. To undermine the unworkable practices of living into which he has drifted and substitute for them others that are effective and satisfying.

Putting it somewhat differently, the job of therapy is to help the schizophrenic adjust to his illness and to life in general.

THE ACUTE PSYCHOTIC EPISODE

Schizophrenia is regarded as a disease of long duration and insidious onset, so that it is possible frequently to trace back into the childhood of a schizophrenic an emotional problem of some sort, such as clinging behavior, which can in retrospect be construed as the kernel of the full-blown psychosis that appears later. But no such problem is characteristic of schizophrenia, so clinicians have not been able to predict which children will develop the illness later on in their lives. The typical schizophrenic comes to medical attention usually at the time of his first psychotic break.

An acute psychosis represents not just a breakdown of the ordinary patterns of living, but the development of new and extraordinary behaviors which, although unsatisfactory, also have pattern and meaning.

A nineteen-year-old man left home for the first time in his life to attend college. Before then he had given no indication that he was schizophrenic. He had demonstrated no evidence at all of any emotional illness except perhaps for the usual adolescent turmoil manifested by some anxieties about his appearance and by wrangling with his overprotective parents. Once at school, however, he became acutely disturbed. He paced restlessly and went without sleep, and then, after a few days, without food. He talked volubly and, according to a teacher, incoherently. He became angry for no apparent reason, and once he seemed on the verge of striking his roommate. The evening of that day, he was found sitting quietly in a straight chair in a darkened room. He did not answer when spoken to, and did not move. He sat stiffly like a waxen figure exactly in one position throughout the night. The next morning he was carried in that same chair to a hospital. He had not eaten or slept for an indeterminate period of time, and he had not urinated for at least twelve hours.

This immobile state is a form of schizophrenia known as the catatonic type, and although it is only one of a number of clinical types, it demonstrates the extraordinary disruption of behavior and the outpouring of feeling, such as anxiety or rage, that are common to most acute schizophrenic reactions. The resulting condition is not, as it appears to be, chaotic or formless. There is a reason and a purpose to these symptoms. This young man, for example, although entirely unresponsive for days, almost deathlike, was able subsequently to explain his actions:

"I was afraid of losing control and hurting someone. The only way I could be sure of what I was doing, or not doing, was to stay absolutely still. I couldn't even let go of my urine. I couldn't speak, but I heard everything everyone said, and I remember everything."

His behavior, as bizarre as it seemed, was a reasoned, if not reasonable, response to an idea; his idea that there were destructive impulses inside of him, which he could not control and from which he was in deadly danger, is common among schizophrenics. Psychotherapy, in order to be successful, must address itself to such ideas and to the complicated, self-destructive behaviors that grow out of them.

Treatment of the Acute Psychotic Episode

Even before a considered plan of treatment can be devised, *steps must be taken to protect the patient.* An acutely psychotic person requires the care of a psychiatrist and often that of a hospital. The first job of his friends and family, therefore, is to ensure that he is brought to a psychiatrist for evaluation. Usually he himself knows something is the matter with him and will agree to go, if he is told calmly to do so. No one should be embarrassed to recommend professional help for anyone, but certainly not for someone so seriously ill. Like many other illnesses an acute schizophrenia is easier to treat early, before it has progressed and worsened. Sometimes the schizophrenic is already too sick to realize he is sick, and he may object to psychiatric referral. Most of the time he will go anyway with encouragement, but sometimes one of a variety of legal measures must be taken to ensure that he does.

The treatment of an acute schizophrenic psychosis, in the hospital or out, involves, first of all, *the use of medication*. It is hard to exaggerate the effect the major tranquilizers have had on the management and on the course of schizophrenia since their advent less than thirty years ago. The number of schizophrenic patients in mental hospitals at any one time has dropped by over one half. Their typical stay has also dropped from a matter of months and years to a matter of weeks; and when they return home, they are more likely to remain out of the hospital, if they continue taking their medicine. Because of these drugs the patient can rest and sleep, and think more coherently, and so he becomes more accessible to psychotherapy.

Considering that schizophrenics suffer terribly, and considering also that their condition is alleviated very definitely by these drugs, it is odd that many such patients refuse, nevertheless, to take them. Even in the setting of a psychiatric ward, which is presumably closely supervised, a random search will turn up caches of pills that patients have hidden away rather than swallow. This problem becomes aggravated after the patient leaves the hospital. Sometimes he seems least willing to take tranquilizers when he is most disturbed and in need of them. Such perverse behavior has been dismissed simply as self-destructive, but more likely is a response to the side effects of the tranquilizers, some of which are unpleasant. Some patients report, in addition, that the sense of being calm itself is oppressive, as if someone were controlling them or holding them down. Consequently the more medicine these particular patients take, the more agitated they may become. For that reason, the patient's wishes cannot simply be disregarded. They are one factor along with very many others which the psychiatrist must weigh in deciding how much medicine to prescribe. Some patients, if supervised closely, can regulate their own dosage; indeed, some schizophrenics do not need to take medicine at all.

What the tranquilizers can do, more or less, is control the agitation and other physical manifestations of an acute psychosis. To some extent also, they may lessen the disruption of thinking. What they cannot do, however, is everything else. They cannot explain the world to the schizophrenic or compensate for the deficiencies of his past life. Those tasks are part of a supportive psychotherapy. Consider again the catatonic young man described earlier in this chapter.

He was admitted into the hospital and told that he would be cared for. Although he said nothing to indicate that he was listening, he was told that his condition would improve with treatment. He was encouraged to urinate, which he did, and begin eating, which he did the following day. A few days later he began to speak and to move slowly, although disjointedly, like a rusted mechanism that was beginning to unwind. At this point he expressed the thought that another patient, who happened to resemble his father, was able to influence his mind. He had then the uncanny sense of being not wholly himself, but partly that other man. He became frightened that he would find it necessary to strangle this man in order to be free. The nursing staff pointed out to him repeatedly that he was the only person in control of his behavior. He was not subject to anyone's mental influence. Moreover, the other man had no interest in him. He was reminded that even were he to lose control of his angry feelings and strike out, the attendant who was still accompanying him constantly would not permit him to injure anyone else. These remarks were plainly comforting to the young man, who soon reported that these ideas were no longer troubling him.

Although acutely psychotic, the schizophrenic can be reassured. He must realize first of all that his condition, which may seem bizarre to him, is familiar to the people taking care of him, and treatable. His pain will be more tolerable once he understands that there is a way for him to get better. But he can be reassured also in other ways. Having unrealistic, sometimes fantastic ideas, he needs someone to point out to him what is real. If he is worried about his physical health, his identity drifting away, his friends hating him, the end of the world coming, or, as this young man was, being influenced telepathically, he needs someone to point out what is really happening. A simple statement of the truth repeated, perhaps, from time to time is helpful.

On the other hand it is not helpful to someone so disturbed to hear a casual explanation of his unconscious mind. Perhaps in this case a psychiatrist could have surmised that the fear this young man had of the other patient, and the rage, had to do really with feelings he had toward his own father, whom that other patient resembled. He might, then, have said something to that effect, but such a remark would not have been reassuring. It would have been tantamount to saying that the patient wanted to strangle his father. Besides, someone so ill is unable to pay attention to such emotionally laden remarks. He is likely to misunderstand, hear one fragment or another out of context, or hear things that were not said at all. The patient's inner life does not need to be explained to him while he is in the midst of an acute psychosis. It is reality that needs to be described.

The disturbed schizophrenic has other needs to which therapy must address itself. If he is anxious and upset, he must be calmed. If he cannot eat or sleep, he must be helped to do these things. If he is isolated, he must be drawn back into the company of others. If he has not tended to his physical well-being, someone must do that for him. If he cannot control himself, or thinks he cannot, external controls must be provided in his environment, whether they are in the form of a regular daily routine to which the patient can apply himself, or in the more obvious form of a constant attendant who watches him, or even a locked room into which he can go to feel safe from himself. In short, someone must compensate for all the impairments in functioning brought on by the psychotic process, whether those deficiencies are psychological, social or physical.

Some of these deficiencies are obvious, but some other needs the schizophrenic may have are not always easy to discover. He is often so preoccupied that he seems to be off in his own world, unable or unwilling to communicate his feelings. Sometimes, because of his thought disorder he seems to be using language in order to obscure rather than make plain what he is thinking. *In order to understand the schizophrenic, then, the therapist must listen carefully.* The loose associations that characterize schizophrenic thought are not without meaning. Ideas are connected only tangentially, but they are connected. A therapist who is sensitive, or who is very in tune with a particular patient, will be able to comprehend him.

In trying to communicate with the patient, the therapist should not talk to him as the patient himself talks—in "schizophrenese." Rather, he should be a model of rational thinking. There is a sane purpose that underlies the confused communications and behavior of the schizophrenic, and that purpose should be addressed rationally in ordinary, simple speech. But more important to the schizophrenic than the need to communicate particular feelings and thoughts is the act of communication itself. It is a step away from his isolation and loneliness. Also, in the process of communicating, he may first begin to understand himself, for talking with another person helps him to organize his ideas into intelligible form.

PARANOID SCHIZOPHRENIA

The tendency of the schizophrenic to misconstrue the world is most striking in the paranoid form of schizophrenia, the form most commonly diagnosed. Someone so affected has become convinced that events in the world at large have some special purpose with respect to him, or that people are treating him in some special way, usually intending to do him some harm. Such an idea is called a delusion, and is often accompanied by auditory hallucinations, imaginary voices that may be accusing or threatening. Other sorts of delusions and hallucinations are possible, but the following case history may be taken as typical.

A twenty-four-year-old man was promoted at work. Shortly thereafter he noticed that his former colleagues, to whom he was now senior, began looking at him enviously. He had the feeling they were talking about him behind his back, and once or twice he caught them laughing together. Also he began to notice that strangers would look at him from across the street and laugh, or signal peculiarly with their hands. Finally he decided that the cars driving on the parkway that went by his house were sent to spy on him. He locked himself in the bathroom and came out only after the police were called.

He was admitted to a hospital, where he became more disturbed. Noises in the plumbing seemed to him to be voices muttering. Occasionally when he was alone, he heard a man's voice calling him names. He became convinced that the hospital staff was part of a plot that included his employer and certain members of his family, the purpose of which was to deprive him of his livelihood and make him helpless.

Unfortunately this man lived in a state which had recently passed laws making it difficult to give medication involuntarily to psychotic persons, with the result that he remained seriously ill for months.

Other ideas commonly incorporated in delusional systems are:

1. The conviction that the individual is specially chosen, by God perhaps, to fulfill some important purpose.

2. The thought that one's spouse is unfaithful.

3. The thought that certain powerful organizations, the government, the CIA, or the Mafia, have made the affected person the object of a conspiracy.

4. The idea that one is in reality a very important, perhaps famous person or has unique powers, such as the ability to read minds.

5. The idea that one is under the sway of others, who may command every aspect of his behavior.

Such ideas are not fixed upon randomly; they reflect feelings the deluded person has about himself. The paranoid schizophrenic attributes to other people feelings that are really his—rage, for instance, or sexual urges. If he feels angry at his employer, he may consider himself to be the object of his employer's anger. If he feels lust and regards such a feeling as reprehensible, he may project it onto his spouse and become jealous. The spouse becomes the one who is lustful and unfaithful. Sometimes the paranoid idea is a statement of an unconscious feeling in an altered form, transformed, perhaps, into the opposite feeling. A woman who feels worthless may imagine that she is the most important person in the world, specially chosen by God to save the world. In a sense a delusion embodies a wish, just as a dream does, even perhaps as a nightmare does.

Being paranoid is really simply having a readiness to jump to certain conclusions, and is not just characteristic of schizophrenia. Someone who is not psychotic but who is suspicious in manner, or jealous, or resentful and self-important, is said to have a paranoid personality. When something goes wrong, he looks for someone to blame, as if nothing bad ever happened without some malevolent person making it happen. Normal people under stress can become unduly suspicious and seem paranoid.

Nevertheless the schizophrenic, because of his perceptual disorder, is particularly likely to come to a paranoid resolution of his conflicts. He has trouble judging a situation or a relationship; as a result he interprets everything in the world as if it had significance for him. He is like a scientist gone awry, trying to find meaning and explanation where there is none. Someone smiling is presumed to be snickering at him. Ordinary gestures convey a mysterious message about him. Cars driving along a highway have a special purpose and a relevance to him. In retreat from a sense of being unimportant, the paranoid schizophrenic imagines himself at the center of a beneficent or a malignant attention. As the result, though, he frightens himself and feels still worse.

The hallucinations that are often associated with a paranoid delusion are another result of the inability of the schizophrenic to separate his inner self from an outer reality. They are the tangible effect of an idea on a perception. In contrast to the voices heard by someone with a brain tumor—which are likely to be random sounds or phrases—the hallucinations of the schizophrenic have content. Someone who feels he is being persecuted is likely to hear threatening voices. Someone who thinks he has been singled out by God is likely to hear God's voice telling him so. In a sense it is his own voice that the schizophrenic hears.

The paranoid schizophrenic may not pay attention properly

to the real events of his life, but he pays very close attention, indeed, to any circumstance, to any nuance of anyone's behavior, that would serve to justify his delusions. Any stray comment is misheard and misconstrued as corroborating evidence. For that reason he may be acutely aware of facts to which everyone else is oblivious. A paranoid individual is sensitive in certain ways and as a result may be drawn to certain professions.

The wife of a police detective obtained a court order that required her husband to submit at once to a psychiatric examination. She had reported to the judge that her husband was pathologically jealous. He accused her of having sexual relations with a neighbor. He followed her when she went shopping and lurked about in the shrubbery when she stayed home. He tapped his own phone illegally and occasionally broke in on his wife's conversations. Recently he had taken an interest in the laundry and in the household accounts and in other ways was behaving peculiarly so that his wife was becoming afraid of him. Otherwise she thought his behavior was ridiculous.

Her husband confirmed this account to the psychiatrist. He explained that he examined the household accounts in order to discover any special expenditures such as might be used to pay for extra clothes or cosmetics or extra visits to the beauty parlor. He inspected the laundry, and in particular his wife's underwear, in order to look for stains that could be interpreted as direct evidence of a sexual excitement. Finally, every day after returning from work, he measured the level of ice in the refrigerator. "If three or four cubes are lower or higher than the others, it means that they were used in drinks for my wife and my damned neighbor, and then the tray was filled up again," he explained.

At the end of the interview the psychiatrist, who thought

that the man was a paranoid schizophrenic, suggested to him that he ought to go into treatment, giving as a reason his obvious emotional distress.

"You would be upset too, if your wife was having an affair," the man replied heatedly.

The psychiatrist pointed out that despite all of the spying that the detective had done, he had uncovered no real evidence that his wife was, in fact, having an affair—and anyway, even if she were, his reaction was excessive. Jealousy of the proportion he had been suffering is never simply a response to infidelity. The psychiatrist went on to say that obviously anyone who measures the ice in his refrigerator as a clue to a possible sexual liaison is doing something that is on the face of it abnormal.

The detective rose stiffly from his seat. "Doctor, you may know something about psychiatry, but you don't know anything about detective work," he announced indignantly, probably with some justice, and he stalked out of the room.

Being paranoid is no advantage, even for a detective. Such a person may be aware of a world of detail that has escaped the notice of everyone else, but not every detail in the world is relevant. Even when there is a kernel of truth underlying his delusion, as there is sometimes, he is likely to become preoccupied with that single fact to the exclusion of all others. A paranoid schizophrenic's focus of attention is at the same time both too narrow and too broad. When he becomes acutely psychotic, these tendencies are aggravated, and he becomes lost among a host of tiny circumstances that add up in his mind to facts of overwhelming significance.

The paranoid schizophrenic, then, is a complicated person who may have unusual sensitivities and intelligence. These qualities can be turned to his advantage and utilized in the process of treatment to compensate for the singular deficiencies of judgment that are also his and that are described above.

Before he can help himself, however, he must be helped by someone else past the immediate problems of his life.

Because the paranoid schizophrenic is confused about the meaning of events in his life, someone must undertake to explain those events to him. If he thinks he is being persecuted at work, for instance, a therapist or a family member or someone else must help him to examine that idea critically. First of all that person must listen to the patient carefully, without prejudice and without contempt. Just as a hypochondriac cannot be reassured about his health without first being examined physically, a paranoid individual will not be reassured by someone who has not first given serious attention to what he has to say. A facile and uninformed assertion that the patient's worries are unfounded will not comfort him. If he were so willing to believe people, he would not be paranoid to begin with. Only when the patient is convinced that someone has really examined his ideas and understands them will he consider that person's opinion and be subject to his influence. Of course the patient should not then be humored. Sometimes a paranoid individual begs for confirmation of his suspicions in order to know the worst, once and for all. Lying to him, however, does not pacify him and is likely to cause more trouble.

A highly imaginative, although suspicious, man in his mid-thirties, a television producer, accompanied his wife one day to the dentist. He sat patiently while his wife was examined in the next room. Occasionally he heard the sounds of laughter penetrate through the door. He was struck by the lascivious quality of the laughter, and the suspicion grew suddenly within him that his wife and her dentist were having a sexual affair. Later on, when he accompanied his wife home, he confronted her with this accusation. She was indignant. She had laughed, she said, because her dentist had told a joke. He had a good sense of humor, she said. Nevertheless her husband's suspicion was unrelieved. He began to watch his wife carefully, as if she would betray her feelings somehow in her expression or in a casual remark. And he made arrangements to accompany her to her next dental appointment. At that visit he sat anxiously in the waiting room, listening to his wife laugh quietly, almost sardonically. At other times she fell strangely silent, and the only sound he could hear was the hum of the dental drill.

During the next week this unfortunate man tormented his wife and himself with endless suspicions. He told her that he would understand if she had been unfaithful, but he had to know for sure. If only he knew definitely, he would forgive her; but his wife continued to protest her innocence. However, he badgered her so constantly that finally she called up her dentist and explained the situation. She asked him for permission to tell her husband, just to quiet him, that they had indeed been intimate, but that the affair was all over now. The dentist became outraged, of course, and refused. Nevertheless the woman decided the only way to comfort her husband was to confess to this imaginary relationship. When she did so, her husband fell silent at once, but at the next dental appointment he came up to the dentist and attacked him with his fists. The dentist promptly initiated court proceedings against the man and his wife.

No one, not the patient's family nor his therapist, should overtly or tacitly encourage the patient's delusional view of the world, which is distorted, after all, and often terrifying.

On the other hand neither should the therapist argue with the paranoid patient. It seems odd that any person will hold stubbornly to a frightening delusion, but the schizophrenic constructs such an idea to make sense out of his confused perceptions, which otherwise seem to him chaotic and still more frightening. Consequently he may object strenuously to any contradiction of his paranoid ideas. In some cases the delusion itself is comforting, although the state of mind of the deluded person is otherwise distressed. Luckily the patient can begin to improve without giving up his delusion immediately. Sometimes he can do well enough without giving it up at all.

A twenty-nine-year-old woman who entered a hospital suffering from a full-blown paranoid psychosis was discharged three months later, in all obvious respects normal except for the idea that she had been chosen by God to do His work. She joined a church where she was honored as a holy person. Her husband reported to her psychiatrist months later that she was "better now than when I married her." And everyone else seemed to agree.

A delusion by itself, without the other elements of the schizophrenic process, may not be destructive of someone's life if it does not seem peculiar to the people around him and does not for that reason serve to isolate him.

A delusion does not usually appear full-blown and unheralded. The schizophrenic is likely to feel first a vague uneasiness. He may have a sense of something odd going on, which then progresses to a formless worry, and only then to a conviction that something specific—usually something bad—is happening to him. The sudden resolution of these disturbing ambiguities into certainty may provide a temporary feeling of relief, even exhilaration. Then in time, if the patient improves, his conviction may recede once again into doubt and uncertainty; if he recovers completely, he will completely abandon such ideas, which may seem to him then to be absurd. And yet still later on he may once again become strikingly paranoid. At least during those stages of this reversible process when he is unsure of himself, he is subject to the influence of other people. Then the therapist should say to him straight out what is real—what the truth is, if he knows what the truth is. The patient may be told that he is not being spied upon or controlled by others. At such times he can be reassured to an extent.

Just as a paranoid schizophrenic is confused about the meaning of events in the world, he is similarly confused by the meaning of his own behavior and feelings and thoughts. *The therapist, therefore, should try, as well as he can, to explain the patient to himself.* That explanation should be simple. The schizophrenic does not need so much to understand the roots of his personality as the gist of his day-to-day existence. He may need to know, for instance, that his angry feelings at a particular moment are related to what someone has just said to him. Or if he behaves irrationally, he may be better able to control that behavior when someone can explain to him the purpose of it. Yelling at a parent, for example, may be due to a fear of abandonment or resentment of some other authority. A distorted perception such as a hallucination may be understood similarly as an expression of a fear or a wish. God's voice proclaiming the importance of the patient to the world may be related reasonably and sometimes convincingly to the patient's feeling of helplessness. In such a way, over a period of time, the schizophrenic may come to understand himself.

Although the patient should be encouraged to be frank with his therapist, he should be told not to share his ideas with other people; for to a considerable extent, his well-being will depend on what others think of him. A man can privately suspect his employer of persecuting him as part of a Communist plot, but he cannot mention it to anyone at work, for he will surely be fired. Similarly, a man may live with the secret knowledge that Doomsday will arrive next month in the shape of a great flood, but if he begins to build an ark in his backyard, his neighbors will sooner or later become uneasy, and he will be committed to an institution. Someone who voices such ideas is likely to be regarded as dangerous.

Sometimes the patient is unable to keep his ideas to himself even when instructed to do so. He is so enthralled by his delusion that he cannot recognize the strangeness of it, and he tells everyone. His inability to keep his thoughts to himself is an indication of his general lack of self-control, which in turn is an indication of his need for external controls. A man who has conceived that there is a plot against him may possibly be treated as an outpatient, but if he has acted on his delusion by confronting the person he suspects, or by calling the police, or by purchasing a weapon, he has become dangerous and should be hospitalized. Paranoid schizophrenics do not usually become violent, but there are exceptions. Consequently their ideas, and their aggressive thoughts particularly, must be monitored closely. If a patient is convinced that he must protect himself by force, then he must be protected against himself. Left unattended he may decide that his only recourse is to a weapon; and so he may shoot someone.

But a paranoid schizophrenic may be destructive in more subtle ways. He may destroy his marriage. He may punish and neglect his children. Someone who treats such a patient, therefore, must make sure that he understands what is really happening in that person's life. He must ask the family specifically about the patient's persecutory ideas, and about any secretive or impulsive behavior that he may have shown. Often he must visit the patient's home to see for himself.

Of course the therapist should not place himself in a position where he himself may be injured by the patient, and neither should anyone else. Such an event, when it occurs, is always upsetting to the patient and no good for the other person. If a patient is in a rage, he should be left alone. If he is in an uncontrollable rage, other people should be called, perhaps the police. In the face of overwhelming numbers he is likely to calm down quickly.

5 THE LONG-TERM TREATMENT OF THE SCHIZOPHRENIC: THE PROCESS OF SOCIALIZATION

THE unawareness the schizophrenic has of himself and of the world in general stems in part from a profound withdrawal which is thought by some to be the central phenomenon of the schizophrenic process. Withdrawing from everyone when he becomes anxious, the schizophrenic retreats into fantasy; the more isolated he becomes, the more fantastic is his vision of the world. He sees everyone distorted by the prism of his unconscious mind. His feelings take shape as delusions and hallucinations and other phantoms. If his isolation becomes chronic, the fabric of his entire life begins to unravel. He forgets how to be a person in a particular society. He forgets exactly how to behave in the role of a man or a woman, or a parent, or a friend. He no longer knows how to work. His ability to care for himself may falter, to the extent that he no longer dresses or washes properly. He forgets how other people expect him to be. Neither does he know what to expect from them. The most commonplace things they say seem peculiar to him and full of special and hidden meanings, and every additional remark seems to be further corroboration of his suspicions. He grows further apart from them and from the ordinary commerce of life. And as he drifts away from everyone else, he becomes set in his own eccentric ways.

A young man walked hesitantly into the offices of a community psychiatric clinic, backed out, walked in sideways again, took a few steps to the left, another few steps forward and a few steps to the right, then sat down. The people sitting next to him immediately moved away. They might have reacted to him similarly even had he not made such an uncommon entrance, because his appearance was strange. His hair was uncombed and grew in scraggly patches down to his chin. He had on sunglasses which were altogether black. He wore a flannel shirt and two sweaters, short pants, and loafers with socks that had drifted down under his ankles. He was nineteen years old.

His symptoms were too varied and waxed and waned too widely to describe in a short passage—but they included the following:

1. A fear of "glinty" surfaces, which might reflect light into his eyes, hurting them. For that reason he looked away from buildings and cars because their windows might catch the sunlight. He was also afraid his eyes might be damaged by looking into the bigger eyes of animals.

2. He was afraid his ears would be hurt by listening to loud sounds or to threatening words. He felt uncomfortable with strangers, for he could not anticipate what words they might say. He stayed at home as much as he could to avoid the sounds of traffic. He could not shave with an electric razor because of its noise.

3. He worried about giving the right coins to bus drivers—

not the right change, but the right coins. If he had the choice of different quarters, he felt them over and over, trying to tell which quarter he should give up. No matter how much he worried ahead of time, however, he usually felt afterward that he had made the wrong decision.

4. He was worried about carrying packages or a briefcase because the extra weight might hurt the soles of his feet. He went monthly to a podiatrist, who contrived to perform some procedure or other on his feet despite their being perfectly normal.

5. He had similar concerns about his nose and other organs of his body, especially his penis, which he had never touched or washed—"for safety's sake."

6. He could not bear to close a door while someone was talking on the television set, lest the conversation be cut off in midsentence.

7. He was peculiarly subject to the influence of other people. If he heard a commercial telling him to buy gum, he felt compelled to buy gum. If he did not, the words came back to haunt him throughout the day. If he did buy the gum, he felt obligated to throw it away unused, because otherwise his teeth might fall out.

8. He could not sit comfortably in one chair when he had the choice of others. He bounced from one to the other, looking for the "right chair." He had been suspended from college because he would not sit still.

9. He heard voices telling him to walk backward or sideways. Recently, conflicting voices commanded him in different directions, so that proceeding very far in any given direction was becoming impossible.

These various complaints and others had led him to spend his days in his room, closed off from any distressing encounter with the world. He talked to no one outside of his immediate family, which included a mother and two sisters, all of whom were schizophrenic. His father had vanished a number of years before while going out for a pack of cigarettes. The patient had come to treatment at last because he had received notice to report for induction into the army, and he thought that he might not be able to perform the duties of a soldier effectively.

This extremely disturbed and detached young man was by no means a typical schizophrenic: he was much worse. But the treatment he received demonstrates those principles that govern the treatment of every schizophrenic, whether he is acutely psychotic or in relative remission. The goal of treatment is to return him into the company of other people, for he suffers above all from being alone. Besides, everything that is worthwhile in life has to do with other people.

The therapist begins by offering himself as a person to whom the schizophrenic can relate. This relationship is akin to that between friends, and also to that between parent and child, and between teacher and pupil; yet it is somehow more than any of these, because the therapist can step back and forth among these roles. He is conscious of how he represents himself to the patient. If at one point he acts firmly as a parent would, to prevent his patient from doing something dangerous or potentially harmful, it is not out of a fixed inclination to be autocratic, but out of an appreciation that the patient's need at that point is for someone like a parent. The patient, knowing that, comes to feel secure. At a different time the therapist will encourage his patient to be assertive and independent. Indeed, being independent is possible only when someone already feels secure. But the therapeutic relationship is hard to characterize simply, probably because what passes between people is always complicated. Whatever else may go on, however, the therapist must have a genuine affection for and interest in his patient, and they both must respect each other.

Schizophrenics do not always engender such feelings. They communicate poorly, and so they are hard to know. They may also be unpleasant, hostile, or threatening, or infantile and clinging. Invariably they are troublesome. They are people with rough edges, hard to seize upon. The warm feelings that therapists do come to feel toward their schizophrenic patients are a triumph of the natural tendency of one person to like another. However it is not natural for everybody to like everybody else. Should a psychiatrist, or someone else acting in the role of therapist, discover that he does not like a particular patient for whatever reason, he should, without feeling guilty or embarrassed, give up that treatment to someone else as soon as he can. Since the schizophrenic is likely to provoke anyone, under the best of circumstances he will surely provoke someone who does not like him very much to begin with—to the point where that person may rupture their relationship. When a therapist sees a patient for six months or a year, he becomes a repository for that person's hopes. If he then chooses not to see him anymore, he has given him one more reason for not trusting anyone, and he has made any subsequent treatment by anyone else much harder. *In order for treatment to be effective, it has to continue for a very long period of time, at least for years.* The schizophrenic needs to know that even when he is at his very worst, he is tolerable to other human beings. He needs to learn that even someone who knows the worst about him can still care about him.

This particular schizophrenic man entered into treatment and saw the same therapist on a weekly basis for the next six years. Although he was remarkably improved at the end of that time, he obviously needed to be in treatment still. Very possibly he would need to call or see his therapist intermittently for the rest of his life.

The therapeutic relation is by itself a counter to the isolation of the schizophrenic process; but more important it is the lever with which the therapist can influence his patient to behave differently, to change.

The patient will respond, to a degree, to persuasion. This young man was led, literally, by his therapist out of his room and into the world. They went on walks together. In such a concrete way the therapist demonstrated that the world was safe. Nothing was so frightening that it required him to avert his eyes, and no remark was so threatening it could not be listened to. He encouraged his patient, and later on, when their relationship allowed him more authority, he instructed him, to ignore the voices that ordered him in different directions, and to ignore commercials and advertisements, however insistent they seemed to be. He told him also to shave, to dress appropriately to his age, to use whatever seat was immediately before him and whatever change came immediately to his hand—without permitting himself to consider other possibilities or to change his mind. In short he was told not to give in to every contrary impulse. And he was told to do what was obviously best for him. Of course, he had been told something similar many times before by many other people, without being able to comply. For example, since he was small, his mother had told him over and over to leave the house, but her motives were different. Rather than encouraging him to be independent, she was threatening him, for she too was afraid of the world. Besides, although she told him regularly to get out, she told him just as often to stay, and to stay forever, because she needed him to take the place of his father, who had run away. The message his therapist communicated was much less complicated, contradictory, and self-serving. Also his therapist knew him well enough to know his strengths and weaknesses, how much anxiety he could tolerate, and consequently how much progress he could make, and how fast.

Within a few months this man could walk in a straight line; he shaved, and he dressed normally. Consequently he could no longer be recognized at first glance as psychotic—which was a fact of overwhelming significance to his life. He was no longer derided by children in the street or avoided by everyone he met. If still he could not make friends, at least he could make acquaintances. A process of socialization had begun.

Necessarily in the course of treatment the therapist advises the patient on how to conduct his life, without, however, taking control of it. This fine line is difficult to draw, especially because the same patient may at different stages of his illness require different amounts of supervision.

This young man, at the beginning of treatment, needed to be instructed in every area of his life, including when to eat and sleep. Left to his own devices he would not eat over an entire weekend, in order not to injure his teeth; he could not, or would not, sleep, because he was disturbed by the sounds of his mother breathing in the next room. Following such periods of sleeplessness he became worse. This is frequently the case with schizophrenics. Therefore proper care of an acutely ill schizophrenic must include attention to such ordinarily self-regulating body functions as eating and sleeping. Fortunately these are usually temporary problems only. Two years later, when this man was improved, such a regulation on the part of the therapist was unnecessary and would have seemed a grotesque imposition.

In order to bring the schizophrenic more closely into contact with other people, the therapist must explain their behavior to him. Society is governed, down to the last particular, by conventions so much a part of everyone's life that they are never openly articulated, except perhaps to children. An ordinary conversation, for instance, is conducted in compliance with unspoken rules that determine who may speak and for how long, and which subjects are suitable for discussion in which groups. These rules go on to proscribe certain activities such as belching or passing wind or coughing openly in someone's face. But operating also are other, unspecified rules which determine, among other things, how closely one may stand or sit to other people, how loudly one may speak, which gestures or movements are meaningful or at least neutral and which others are a distraction, and so on. Some of these rules vary among different cultures; others are surprisingly constant from place to place and go unnoticed until violated by someone who is so grossly disturbed that he is unaware of them.

This man was as strange to the people of Chicago, the city in which he lived, as if he had come from another planet; and they seemed as strange to him. He did not know what they meant when they smiled at him or were friendly to him, or when they asked him simple questions, or when they ridiculed him. If a shopkeeper recommended to him a particular brand of soap, he wondered what the shopkeeper really meant, and wondered also whether that recommendation had the force of a commandment or could be safely ignored. Day by day his therapist had to translate for him the ordinary behavior of ordinary people. At the same time, he was teaching him painstakingly how to act in public, for this man had to learn, at the age of nineteen, how to greet someone and how to say good-bye and how to behave during the thousand little encounters of life. He had to learn, for instance, the conventions of traveling on a bus: the procedures for standing in line, how to respond when someone touched him or told him to move ahead, how to ask directions of the bus driver, how much room to occupy when sitting down, where to stand in order to be out of everyone's way, and how to get off the bus without colliding with people or offending them. His therapist encouraged him as he threaded his way through these intricacies, and congratulated him upon his successes. He helped him to accept his failures as temporary. Sometimes he interceded on his patient's behalf with teachers and other people of significance in his life, so that they too could be enlisted in helping him. As time went on, his therapist explored with him the possibility of working and then guided him through the process of applying for, then holding on to, a job. Still later, and probably hardest of all, he helped his patient to venture forth into heterosexual relationships.

In our pluralistic society there are surprisingly rigid rules governing the way men and women relate to each other. This therapist had to explain the social conventions governing dating and the proper way to approach a girl sexually. As if he were making that explanation to a child, he had to go slowly and tactfully, more responding to questions than volunteering information. If a therapist propels his patient prematurely into a sexual confrontation, he will only frighten him. On the other hand the therapist should be open and not made anxious himself by the discussion of sexual issues.

This patient was bizarre in appearance and behavior, whereas most schizophrenics are ordinary. He was incompetent at school, at work, and in his relationship with other people, whereas most schizophrenics manage pretty well, except perhaps during the period when they are acutely ill. Nevertheless, like this young man, most schizophrenics have problems coping in all these areas. A man may not know how to respond when his boss criticizes him. A woman may tend to withdraw into herself when a girl friend goes someplace without her. Another woman may be troubled by ordinary remarks made to her at a cocktail party. In all these situations, the therapist is helpful: guiding, reassuring, and encouraging.

In part the schizophrenic learns how to behave by modeling himself after his therapist. The therapist represents, it is hoped, an example of a healthy individual. And his relationship with the patient is also a model—of what the patient may expect from other people. The therapist demonstrates that two people may respect each other, despite disagreeing, and like each other and trust each other, even though they are different.

THE ROLE OF THE FAMILY

The chief relationships of the schizophrenic are those that exist between him and members of his family. *Therapy, therefore, takes place in the family setting.*

Volumes have been written about the schizophrenic and his family. Life in their home has been described as "emotionally impoverished," "distorted," "affectively dead," and worse. The parents are blamed usually. The mother is depicted as nagging, anxious, overprotective, and hostile; the father as passive, weak, and isolated. Both are supposed to be unsure of their sexual identities. Frequently the two of them are at odds, it is said, over one issue or another, and other members of the family tend to be drawn into their struggle. Both parents, but particularly the mother, are thought to communicate in a special garble marked by contradiction and irrelevance, not unlike the language of the schizophrenic. Indeed, anyone who sits in on a conversation of such a family is likely to come away struck by the extraordinary ability of everyone to miss the point.

PATIENT (a young woman): I feel sick. I feel terrible. I'm never going to get out of this hospital. I'm going to die here. My body will rot away.

THERAPIST: You will have to be here for a while; but then you will certainly get better and return home.

MOTHER: She never wanted to live at home when she went to college. Her room was a mess.

FATHER (to daughter): You're so egotistical. Do you know every other word out of your mouth is "I"?

Insensitive and irrelevant remarks such as these cause the schizophrenic to withdraw into his own private thoughts. As conversation, they make a discordant sound that is painful to the therapist, who listens to it for an hour at a time, let alone to someone who hears it all his life. The disorders of thought that schizophrenics suffer have been attributed to these peculiarities of communication within their families.

Still, the behavior of a schizophrenic cannot be so reliably explained by his upbringing. Certainly there are parents so brutal and bizarre that their children are predisposed to developing emotional disturbances, and perhaps schizophrenia, but there are some children who grow up apparently normal even under those circumstances. And others who have grown up in warm, supportive families do become schizophrenic.

The parents of schizophrenics are maligned particularly for overprotecting their children, for keeping them infantile; but, of course, they have had to cope over the years with their children's incapacities and tendency to retreat into helplessness. It becomes understandable, therefore, when their need to protect them leads them too far, and they become overprotective. In other ways family behavior is determined sometimes by the behavior of the schizophrenic, rather than the other way around. Yet not all parents respond the same way. Some of these families are in constant storm, while others are played-out and lifeless. And some are not recognizably disturbed at all.

In order for the schizophrenic to become well, his family must learn new ways of responding to him. First they have to pay attention to him. He will turn out to be a somewhat different person than they think he is, troubled in ways they might not have expected, impelled by complicated feelings and thoughts. And if he has become acutely psychotic, or is recovering from an acute psychotic episode, he may be depressed and have special needs. Later on he will require progressively less moment-to-moment attention and will be able to take more responsibility for himself. Determining just how much he can do for himself is difficult and is an important task to which his primary therapist, at this stage in his illness likely to be a psychiatrist, addresses himself—but on the basis, largely, of information provided by the family.

The therapist and the patient's family, therefore, must work together. They should feel free to talk to him, keeping in mind that because of his obligation to respect his patient's confidences, he may not be able to respond as openly as he would like. Still, they shouldn't hesitate to say what they want to him, to complain, if they feel so inclined, or to ask for advice dealing with those crises that seem to grow up naturally in the process of living with a schizophrenic. It is to be hoped that, with the therapist as intermediary, the patient and his family can learn to communicate more effectively among themselves, not blaming each other for everything that goes wrong. Some families are so private that the schizophrenic who grows up in their midst comes to regard people as devious and full of ulterior purpose—which is the paranoid ideology.

The therapist, for his part, needs to know the thousand details of his patient's life, which in sum make up his adjustment. The family is the best source of this information. Some particular behaviors, which may strike the therapist as grave, may turn out to be an accustomed habit of his patient and, therefore, not a significant indicator of how well he is doing, while other actions that may seem unremarkable at first glance may be important. The family can place the patient in context.

The therapist needs to talk to the family for a host of other reasons. He tries to know, and to help the family know, which issues really matter to the well-being of his patient and which are extraneous. Take for example the particularly disturbed young man just described in these pages. It mattered that he dressed so strangely that people moved away from him, for in such a way he became more isolated; it did not matter, on the other hand, that he changed his undershorts only once a week. And yet his mother seemed to care as much about one as the other. She had to be urged many times to give up her interest in his underwear and to expend whatever influence she had on her son more usefully. And it turned out she was able to help him. Although he strained against her authority and was frequently in a rage at her, he did indeed listen to her. With her encouragement he began shaving and dressing more conventionally, like a man rather than a boy. He responded also, at least a little, when she suggested that he spend more time with other people and less time secluded in his room, which was not easy advice for her to give, since deep down she too found people threatening.

The therapist has to guide the family so that they don't ask too much from the patient. No one changes quickly, least of all someone so disturbed. This man, for instance, could not one day step out of his room and to the center of an active, healthy life. He could not respond to his mother's intermittent demands that he "get a job tomorrow, or else!" But he was able, with encouragement, to leave his room on a particular day, for an hour. And he was willing, after a while, to sit in the park, even though he worried that the sun might hurt his eyes. Such short-range goals were within his reach. Later his mother instructed him, somewhat against her better judgment, that he could go out at night also, despite the risk of being mugged; and he did so. First he took short walks. In time he progressed to meeting people briefly, at public lectures where he could be with others and still be mostly by himself. Then he went to social groups run under the auspices of aftercare programs of psychiatric hospitals. The only people he met there were themselves emotionally disturbed, but perhaps for that reason they were willing to put up with him despite his obvious peculiarities. Still later he went to ordinary mixers. Throughout, he was encouraged to be with the healthiest people who would tolerate him, for they were the people from whom he could learn the most. After three years he was able to move out of his mother's home, and from there to the YMCA—and from there to an ordinary apartment which he shared with an ordinary roommate. When he wanted to give up and return home, which was frequently, his mother, again at the urging of his therapist, allowed him to come back, but just briefly. Then she sent him out again, although still not without misgivings. There came a time, finally, when she even encouraged him to go out with girls despite her fears of venereal disease and germs.

The therapist and the family must act in concert to encourage the patient to be independent, yet allow him those moments when he needs to lean on them. They must encourage him without dominating him, interest themselves in his life without being intrusive, and love him without smothering him. The schizophrenic has special needs that are opposite to each other and that seem to exist at the same time, such as the need to be cared for and the need to be left alone. Such precise needs are not easy to satisfy, yet they underlie much of his behavior and sometimes set the course of his life.

Finally it must be kept in mind that although the patient cannot be sacrificed for the sake of his family, made into a scapegoat for everyone else's problems, neither should the family be sacrificed to him. However important the welfare of one person may be, and however sick he may be, he cannot be allowed to use all of his family's time and resources. If his presence is destructive, arrangements should be made for him to live elsewhere, perhaps in a halfway house. One legitimate reason for hospitalizing a patient is to give his family a rest. But that hospital stay then must be as brief as possible.

PROGNOSIS

The course and outcome of schizophrenia depend on a number of factors. A good prognosis, in the context of schizophrenia, implies the following:

1. The likelihood of an acute psychotic episode remitting relatively quickly, perhaps in a matter of a few weeks.

2. The likelihood that acute psychotic episodes in the future will also be of short duration and few in number, or none at all.

3. The likelihood that the life of the schizophrenic between

psychotic episodes will be happy and marked by those successes in work and in relationships with other people that characterize happy lives.

Some of the factors that correlate with a good prognosis are these:

1. A rapid onset of illness. The more rapid and more striking and florid the illness, the better the prognosis. The more insidious the onset, the more likely is the individual to become chronically ill.

2. The presence at the time of onset of a clearly defined stress. A special achievement, such as graduation, may constitute such a stress. A schizophrenic who decompensates for little or no apparent reason is more likely to relapse again in the future.

3. Onset in the late twenties or thirties, rather than at a younger age and particularly rather than adolescence. Childhood schizophrenia has still a worse prognosis, but is defined somewhat differently. In fact, it may be another condition altogether.

4. A good pre-morbid adjustment. The higher the level of attainment the schizophrenic has reached before becoming psychotic, the better the prognosis and the more likely he is to return to that level of functioning. Those skills that go into his previous achievements are those precise skills he will need to recover from his illness. Someone, then, who has a good job and who has been able to marry and make friends has a good prognosis.

5. The appearance of strong feelings during the psychotic state. Individuals who are very anxious or depressed, or even enraged, or possibly, at the other extreme, euphoric, do better than those who are phlegmatic and withdrawn.

6. Brief duration of illness. The more recent the onset of schizophrenia, the less time there has been for a fragmentation of personality and a breakdown of customary habits of living. Also there has been less time for the patient and his family

to become cynical about the effectiveness of treatment; for the typical schizophrenic, unfortunately, is likely to have experienced a number of halfhearted and, therefore, ineffectual attempts at treatment over the course of his illness, a typical treatment consisting perhaps of fifteen minutes of desultory conversation offered begrudgingly every few weeks along with a few pills. Such a meager effort reflects a pessimistic view of schizophrenia that communicates itself quickly to the patient. He responds usually by breaking off treatment and stopping his medicine. Not long after, he becomes sick again and starts again with another therapist, who then must cope not only with his patient's illness but the fact of a previous failure of treatment. After three or four or five such failures every therapist is regarded as temporary, and no therapist, however dedicated, can win the trust of his patient.

7. An intact family. A healthy family provides emotional support to its members, such support being particularly important to the schizophrenic. If other members of his family are mentally ill and relatively incapacitated, as is frequently the case, the chances of his recovering completely from his illness are poorer.

8. Certain favorable characteristics of mind. The outcome of psychotherapy is more likely to be successful when the patient is intelligent or talented or skilled in some way, for any skill at all serves to bolster his self-respect and facilitate his adjustment. But the single trait of personality that seems to count most in treatment is motivation. Some people, no matter how much they suffer, are able to struggle with their problems and eventually overcome them, while others who are much less disturbed despair quickly and consequently fail. And no one can explain why one person is motivated and another not.

9. Certain favorable social conditions. Being rich, as usual, is an advantage. Being poor, uneducated, and undernourished is an obstacle in the successful treatment of schizophrenia as it

is in the treatment of alcoholism, drug abuse, or criminality, or tuberculosis or syphilis or practically any other undesirable condition of man.

10. Proper treatment. The schizophrenic may be expected to do well with proper treatment, which includes both the appropriate use of medication and psychotherapy—but especially psychotherapy. The role of the therapist is not simply to listen analytically, but to protect, comfort, persuade, reassure, and explain—to stand between his patient and the world. Without proper treatment, the schizophrenic has a poor chance of doing well, and in time he may come to resemble the caricature presented at the beginning of Chapter 4. Even if he is not continually psychotic, his life may be interrupted by repeated psychotic episodes. The rest of the time he may be suspicious, unfeeling, and withdrawn, a person who has been wasted. With treatment, on the other hand, he may do very well. Even after a number of previous psychotic episodes he may recover so completely that he seems normal to most people—and to all intents and purposes, he is.

George, who was twenty-one years old, came to psychotherapy two months after being discharged from a mental hospital where he had been treated as an inpatient for the third time in the preceding two years, spending a total of six months on a closed ward. His diagnosis each time was paranoid schizophrenia.

His previous life was unremarkable, except for an accident at age seventeen in which he broke his leg. While he was in the hospital, his father died suddenly from a heart attack; nevertheless he lived through this period of stress without showing evidence of emotional disorder.

After graduating from high school, he went to work as a plumber's apprentice and did well until a second apprentice was hired. Within a few weeks George began to notice that this man seemed to look at him "with a funny glance" and occasionally made strange remarks alluding to George's suntan, as if he were insinuating that George, who had red hair, nevertheless had a strain of Negro blood. These encounters seemed to become more frequent in the succeeding days and weeks. George finally became convinced that there was a conspiracy against him at work, led by the foreman and the other apprentices. Consequently he quit his job and joined the army. His tour of duty was brief. He felt better following his enlistment for a few weeks, but then began to notice that the other enlisted men were snickering when he came into the room or signaling to each other by coughing or sneezing. Finally he developed the notion that his sergeant, who was black, wanted to make him black also. During lunch one day he confronted the sergeant with this accusation and threatened him with a knife; as a result, he was admitted to the army station hospital.

At that time, in addition to these strange ideas, he gave evidence of the disturbances of thought and feeling that are the primary signs of schizophrenia. He wandered into reveries from which he could be roused only with difficulty. His thinking was slowed. He started sentences without finishing them, as if the machinery of his mind had broken down in the middle of a thought. Most striking, however, was his entirely wooden expression. He neither smiled nor frowned. Although he reported terrible fears, he spoke of them only in bland accents. And yet somehow there was apparent under that facade, a haunted look.

Most of these symptoms cleared slowly with medication. After a few months he was well enough to be discharged from the hospital, and immediately thereafter he was separated also from the service. His discharge papers recorded his illness as paranoid schizophrenia, existing prior to his period of service. Had he been in the army for years before becoming sick, his illness still would have been regarded as existing prior to his period of service, for schizophrenia was considered by the armed forces to be a permanent defect, like a congenital malformation, which exists even prior to its first manifestation, then goes on forever after.

George returned home, where he lived uneasily with his mother. He was suspicious of the people around him, but not overtly paranoid. He returned to work as a gas station attendant, and to the company of his friends. He went out with girls. After a time he became engaged to a schoolteacher, but then discovered she was having an affair. He became very upset and shortly thereafter psychotic, with symptoms very similar to those he experienced in the army. He was again hospitalized, this time in a municipal hospital, and underwent the same sort of treatment, which resulted once again in his discharge a few weeks later in a state of relative improvement. Six months later this whole sequence of events was repeated a third time.

George sought no psychiatric help during the crucial periods when he was between psychotic episodes, for none of the professional staff who had taken care of him in the various hospitals in which he had spent so many months had impressed on him the importance of doing so. They had, perhaps, suggested in passing that probably when he returned home from the hospital, he should go into therapy, or at least come back to the hospital drug clinic once a month. Perhaps someone went so far as to give him the telephone number of a local psychiatrist or the local mental hygiene clinic, but no one behaved as if it mattered really whether or not he called. Certainly no one went so far as *to make the appointment for him.* No one indicated to the family the importance to his subsequent course of continuing treatment, for George was in everyone's eyes, already, at the age of twenty, a chronic and presumably incurable schizophrenic.

Somehow George nevertheless pulled himself together for a period of time following his last hospitalization. By a stroke of good fortune he met a responsible young woman who had a child by a previous marriage, and they all fell in love with each other. Although he was still unemployed, he promptly married this woman with the expectation, he said later, that the three of them would live happily forever after. Within a month, however, he expressed the fear that his wife was unfaithful to him, just as his previous girl friend had been. He became angry and made threatening remarks to her. She recognized clearly that he was becoming mentally disturbed, and before he became frankly psychotic, she brought him to a psychiatrist for treatment.

Treatment included the use of medication, quickly and in sufficient doses, and that total mobilization described in these pages of all the resources of the patient and his family. George was not hospitalized, but he and his wife were seen by the psychiatrist every day. A week later he was sufficiently improved to be seen every other day. By that time he no longer openly expressed his suspicions or was threatening in manner. The disorder of thought that he demonstrated seemed less obvious. A few weeks later his emotional responses were less stilted and more spontaneous. Within another few months no one could have recognized in him any evidence at all of schizophrenia. His thinking was clear and logical. His feelings varied appropriately with his circumstances as do those of a normal person. The way he lived seemed normal. He was then seeing his therapist twice a week and was not taking any medication. He had returned to his plumbing job and except for a brief and minor episode in which he once again became unduly resentful of a fellow worker, he adjusted well to work. Over the next year he and his wife made new friends, and they bought a new house. Two years later, although continuing to work as a plumber, he began a new business as a roofer and made a success of it. Another year later he and his wife had a child. Throughout all of these important life changes, George remained, if not unaffected, at least not psychotic.

None of these achievements came without struggle, but

they did come. Five years after treatment began, George showed no more evidence of emotional illness than any average person. His single symptom was, perhaps, an unwarranted tendency to be suspicious of people. He continued to visit his psychiatrist once every two months, perhaps simply to assure himself that his therapist was still there if he needed him. The way he put it to this therapist was: "I like to talk to you every once in a while, just to see how you're doing."

Does it make any sense to call George schizophrenic years after he has been free of any sign of that illness? If the term is used to imply that such a person, currently in remission, still has the potential to decompensate as a schizophrenic once again some time in the future, then the answer is yes: experience has shown that such relapses do occur, not invariably but not uncommonly. But the answer is no if the label *schizophrenia* is used casually and prejudicially to refer to the stereotype described at the beginning of Chapter 4. Schizophrenics do not deteriorate inevitably into regressed and helpless people. Not every schizophrenic is curable, or even improvable—just as not every problem has a solution—but a great number of schizophrenics are able with help to lead perfectly satisfactory lives.

Recently in New York, a fifty-year-old schizophrenic man who had been hospitalized continuously in the same institution for the last thirty years was discharged to the community. He was given fifty dollars, which he had earned doing piecework at the hospital at the usual rate of thirty cents an hour, and he was given the address of a halfway house where a room had been obtained for him. For one entire week he traveled the subways and buses of The Bronx, getting lost and lost again. Finally he was picked up by the police, wandering penniless through the streets, and returned to the hospital, a failure of rehabilitation. Yet this man might have done well had someone taken him by hand to his new residence. He simply needed more supervision than was offered to him at this critical point in his life. *The therapy of schizophrenia hinges on attention to such simple problems, which are not, however, so simple that they yield to halfway measures.*

The goal of therapy, therefore, is to return the schizophrenic to ordinary life and to equip him with ordinary social skills so that he may not be so easily stressed and as a result become subject to the catastrophic effects of an acute psychotic reaction. He must be guarded stubbornly against the long-term deterioration of personality that comes from isolation and inattention. He must be enveloped in a systematic program of treatment that will distract him from his preoccupations and focus his attention on real events in the real world, so that he may work and be involved with people. In short, the goal of treatment of the schizophrenic is to make him live more effectively as measured by those same criteria by which any normal person measures his life.

6 DEPRESSION

IN the course of life everyone experiences certain losses, some of more significance than others. Important relationships break apart or change with time, friends drop away, people die. There are, too, changes of circumstance, the loss of a job, perhaps, or the loss of physical health, through illness or accident. Sometimes that loss is of one's own self, as in the loss of self-respect that comes about through rejection or failure or humiliation. The characteristic reaction of most people to any serious loss is a feeling of sadness or depression.

One example of such a feeling is the normal condition of grief, in which a bereaved person adjusts his life over a period of time to being without someone he has loved. The state of mind of such a person is familiar to everyone. He feels sad. He may cry. He is preoccupied and will not interest himself in his business affairs or in his usual pursuits. He may be irritable and find fault with people, or he may complain about his own physical condition. He may sleep poorly. He is uninterested in food. He may feel tired and loath to move, or conversely, hé may become restless. He may not tend to his appearance. His attention is focused on the past rather than on the present, and he makes no plans for the future. He withdraws into himself. During this period he does not appear to be his normal self, yet he would not be regarded by most people as emotionally disturbed. His condition is recognizable as a typical and perhaps even normal state of grief.

Depression, used in this ordinary sense, therefore, refers to a feeling that everyone experiences to a varying degree at some point or another in his life in response to circumstances, and that can be said to be normal. However, the term *depression* is used technically by psychiatrists—although, as usual, vaguely—to refer also to any one of a number of mental illnesses, or, on other occasions, to a complex of symptoms that may or may not be related to a mental illness. In this sense depression is a pathological state of mind and has in common with most other mental disturbances the fact that it appears as an exaggeration of a normal state of mind.

The dividing line is particularly hard to draw in the case of *neurotic depression*. This diagnosis, made more commonly than any other, refers more to an unhealthy attitude than to an illness. Some people are taught at an early age to think badly of themselves; consequently they become unassertive and unsuccessful. They may feel mildly depressed over the course of a lifetime, although often they improve significantly in a long-term psychoanalytically oriented psychotherapy. On the other hand at the other extreme are the *clinical depressions*. These conditions are severe. They have a distinguishable onset, last for weeks or months, sometimes years, then, usually, even without treatment, come to an end. With proper treatment they resolve much more quickly. Such treatment involves not only the use of medication, but the application of the principles of supportive psychotherapy as they have been elaborated in these pages.

The symptoms of a typical severe depression are as follows.

A disturbance of mood. The dominant mood of the depressed patient is sadness, sometimes a profound sadness, "like a black curtain covering me"; "like a heavy weight." It is a feeling usually at its worst in the early hours of the morning, waning somewhat during the course of the day. The aspect of such a person has been described in great detail, as in the following verbatim example drawn from a hospital record:

". . . the main fold of her upper eyelid along the inner third was pulled upward and backward (sign of Veraguth), and her brows were knitted and furrowed into the shape of the Greek letter Omega (the Omega sign) . . ." In other words, this particular patient was sad about the eyes. She was sad all over, the examiner went on to point out, giving equally detailed account of her stooped posture, the slowness of her movements, and the carelessness of her dress.

The condition of being unhappy or sad, which is after all familiar to most people, is for that reason readily recognizable to most people without such minute examination. Yet it is true that some individuals express feelings of sadness without looking sad. Their facial expression may be composed. They may even smile. Conversely there are others who insist they feel fine at the very same time that they are crying. Still others are so agitated that they seem more anxious than depressed, even though their depression may be severe and the cause for their anxiety. Some patients may refuse to admit that they are sad and say instead that they are only nervous or upset. They may be irritable and are often overtly angry. Still, all of these people will show at some point during their clinical course the sad mood that is considered primary to depression.

Disturbances of thought. The thinking of a depressed person is disturbed to a degree that corresponds to his disturbance of mood. If he is only mildly depressed, he may appear to be lucid or perhaps only distracted somewhat. But there are depressions so severe that they amount to stupor, preoccupying the depressed person so severely he is scarcely able to think at all. He speaks slowly, often inaudibly, often repeating the same thoughts, which are usually morbid in content. He is likely to blame himself for events over which he had no control and which may have happened long ago. It is as if he begins by feeling guilty and only then searches through his life for some justification of that feeling. The reasons he gives to explain his conviction that he is a terrible person are so fantastic sometimes as to constitute a delusion. Or he may experience these ideas as a hallucination, as a statement of condemnation spoken aloud by some unseen person. His sense of impending doom may show itself in obsessive concerns about his health. Ordinary stomach distress suggests cancer. And if he does not think he is going to die at once, he may very well feel that he ought to die. Thoughts of suicide are a constant attendant to anyone who is very depressed.

Physical symptoms. The most striking physical change in a depressed person is an alteration in the level of his physical activity, usually a retardation of movement. He sits quietly, head bent, or walks hunched over, arms held stiffly by his sides. He feels tired all the time. Left to his own devices, he may lie in one position, apparently motionless for hours. Other depressed patients, however, show a heightened physical activity. They become restless and agitated. They pace the halls of the hospital, wringing their hands and crying out to anyone who will stop and listen to them. Apparently these two extremes are the two responses one may have to calamity. One person laments and rushes about, while the other sinks into lethargy.

The very depressed person is also likely to suffer a wide variety of nonspecific physical symptoms, which may occur in anyone who is emotionally upset, for whatever reason. Much of the day-to-day practice of the general practitioner is given over to considering these symptoms and ruling out the presence of any underlying organic disease. Among them are fatigue, headache, dizziness, dimming or blurring of vision, trouble swallowing or breathing, palpitations, chest pain or stomach pain, backache, amenorrhea, loss of interest in sex, and so on. Symptoms particularly associated with depression are insomnia, particularly early morning awakening; loss of appetite to the point where there is loss of weight; and constipation. These are sometimes called the vegetative signs of depression.

Disturbances of attitude and behavior. Someone who is very depressed is likely also to be demanding, clinging, manipulative, and complaining; as a result, he is vexatious to anyone around him, particularly to his family. Because he may engage in self-destructive behaviors, such as drinking, he may strike everyone not so much as a depressed person, but as an alcoholic—or if he uses drugs, as a drug addict. Because these conditions, which frequently obscure an underlying depression, are regarded as self-inflicted, he is tendered little sympathy. It is hard, anyway, to sympathize with someone who is depressed for any length of time. He seems so *unreasonable.* And stubborn. He cannot be comforted or coaxed back to good humor. He sulks. Whatever help someone offers him is swallowed up without apparent benefit, or rejected. Consequently he is left increasingly alone. He is frustrating to his family because he seems helpless and hopeless. Everyone begins to blame him for his own plight, and he too blames himself. Inevitably he begins to consider suicide, which is perhaps the most perfect expression of self-hatred and despair.

Plainly, depression is a psychological disease with primarily psychological manifestations. It is surprising, therefore, to discover that its causes are not primarily, or at least not exclusively, psychological.

Mrs. L. was a woman who had already had a long psychiatric history by the time she reentered treatment at the age of thirty-four in the midst of a depression of psychotic proportion. On this occasion, because she was hospitalized in an academic institution, a systematic effort was made to determine the psychological roots of her condition.

However, her childhood was apparently unremarkable. It is true that when she was very small, she chewed her nails, but such a symptom presages no particular problem later on. When she was an adolescent, she seemed shy and worried some about her attractiveness, but not especially, not more, it seemed, than other girls. She seemed to everyone who knew her at that time to be normal, and so she regarded herself. Yet when she was eighteen, for no discernible reason, she became seriously depressed. She cried, expressed ideas of guilt and remorse, and showed to a varying degree many of those symptoms just described as characteristic of a serious depression. And between then and the time she was thirty-four she suffered three similar, distinct depressions of psychotic proportion, usually of such severity that she needed to be in a hospital.

A very detailed history did not reveal to the psychiatrist any information that would explain these recurrent depressions. The death of a parent early in childhood seems statistically to predispose to depression later in life, but she had experienced no such loss. Nor was there any apparent defect of her relationship with her parents. They were not bad to her in any of the ways parents are usually said to be bad. They were not rejecting or demanding, and were not overly strict. They were not overly protective. They were individuals with their own weaknesses, perhaps, and with their own personalities, like everyone else, but they were not unusual at all. Neither was she. She seemed during these early years not to have been troubled by any abnormal need or conflict or circumstance. Of course, since no one grows up without some struggle or difficulty, an imaginative psychiatrist can always find some behavior he can construe in retrospect as a symptom, but this woman seemed singularly free even of such minor problems.

Certainly there was no clue to why she would subsequently become depressed over and over again.

Nor was there any discernible reason why she became depressed at just those times that she did. There was no apparent relationship between the onset of her depressions and events in her family or in the world in general, bad events or good events. Specifically, these episodes did not correlate with her sexual life, visits to her parents, arguments with her husband, illness, her children going to camp or coming back, or any one of the small circumstances that she thought to mention or her psychiatrist thought to ask about.

Of course, a depression need not be set off by something so obvious as an event. A dream, for instance, or a casual comment by a friend, may bring back a distant, painful memory. Even a passage in a book may have some private meaning and provoke a feeling of melancholy, which may then progress, perhaps, to a depression. By such criteria, however, one may relate anything to anything else. In the case of Mrs. L. her depressions could not be seen to be related to anything at all.

What did seem relevant in understanding her condition was the fact that her father and his mother before him had both experienced similar depressions. In retreat from a psychological explanation, therefore, it was possible to consider her depression to be an organic disease, probably genetically determined. Depression in general is so regarded by many psychiatrists, thought to have something to do, perhaps, with a chemical imbalance in the brain. In support of their thesis they mention the great range of organic conditions and even drugs which have as a side effect a depression that is clinically indistinguishable from the spontaneous depression that the psychiatrist usually encounters. Yet it is true also that, in some cases at least, a depression can indeed be precipitated by an unequivocal, psychological event. Apparently the subjective state of mind of the individual is equivalent in some way to the biological state of his brain. Those of philosophical bent have debated endlessly the priority of one or the other, but the debate has proven sterile. The fact is that neither biology nor psychology has explained the phenomenon of depression satisfactorily. The causes of depression, like the causes of schizophrenia, are for the most part unknown.

Depression, therefore, is a condition whose etiology may not be understood but whose clinical outlines are familiar. In one form or another, to a varying degree, depression is a universal experience. Because even in its most severe form it is common, the burden of its treatment cannot be carried exclusively by psychiatrists or other professionals but must be taken up also by others serving as collateral therapists, and by friends and family.

TREATMENTS

As in the case of schizophrenia, the management of a severe or psychotic depression involves both a supportive psychotherapy and the use of medication. Because the antidepressant drugs, and electric shock treatment, which may be used in their place, are so effective, it is reasonable to begin any discussion of treatment with an explanation of their use.

The organic therapies:

Electric Shock Treatment
It was discovered many years ago that passing an electric current through the brain at intervals over the course of a few weeks tended to relieve the symptoms of depression. No one knew why that was so; even now no one really knows why. Unfortunately, like any other form of treatment, electric shock treatment was found to have undesirable side effects. The electric current caused the patient to convulse, so violently he sometimes injured himself. Also his memory of events prior to treatment was affected, at least temporarily,

and his memory for the weeks of treatment was to some extent lost permanently. The experience of receiving shock was so frightening that many patients, and psychiatrists too, regarded such treatment as inhumane. Because of improvements over the years in the way shock is given, there is currently little likelihood of a patient being injured, and the effect on memory too has been ameliorated; but most patients are still afraid of it, of the whole idea of it, perhaps. But the fact is that electric shock treatment works, and is generally safe. Between eighty and ninety-five percent of psychotically depressed patients who are so treated improve in a matter of days or weeks. However, within the last twenty years drugs have been developed that also achieve a high rate of remission. Consequently, most psychiatrists recommend electric shock only when one of the following conditions exists:

1. An unsatisfactory response to a prior and adequate trial of these medications.

2. A contraindication to the use of these medications because they cause a severe reaction in a particular patient, or because, as a result of their side effects, they complicate the management of a concomitant medical illness; for example, prostatic hypertrophy or certain kinds of heart disease.

3. A particular need for quick results, as in an acutely suicidal patient.

4. A history in a particular patient of a good response to electric shock treatments at the time of previous episodes of depression, especially if drugs used at those times were not effective.

Since these circumstances are not common, the great bulk of persons who are psychotically depressed are treated with drugs.

Medication

It is not possible to educate a lay person in the principles that underlie the use of medication, for they are founded on still more fundamental principles of physiology and biochemistry, which are, in turn, the substance of medicine itself. Therefore drugs can be prescribed safely and reasonably only by a physician. However, since any very depressed person is likely to be on some sort of medication, members of his family and other people assisting in his care should know something about those drugs, what they can and cannot do, and what precautions are necessary in their use.

A cursory examination of a psychiatric textbook will indicate that among the drugs felt to have a place in the treatment of depression are:

The major tranquilizers, of which there are about twenty or twenty-five, and which are divided more or less into five families.

The minor tranquilizers, of which there are another half dozen or dozen agents.

Certain hormones, especially the thyroid hormones and perhaps, sometimes, the sexual hormones.

Psychic energizers, such as the amphetamines and other related drugs.

Inorganic salts, such as lithium carbonate.

The so-called antidepressant drugs themselves, which fall into two major classes, each one of which has eight or ten members.

And assorted sedatives and soporifics, including antihistamines, barbiturates, and a number of other drugs.

There are also, naturally, combinations of these drugs.

Each drug has a chemical name, a generic name, and one or a number of trade names—tranquil names like Trancopal or Tranxene®, or placid names like Placidyl.* The physician

---

* Physicians usually order a drug by its trade name even though it is usually more expensive than the same drug ordered by its generic name. Advertising has made the trade names familiar. The physician knows *Librium*® very well, but may not recognize it as Chlordiazepoxide hydrochloride, its generic name. Its chemical name,

chooses among these drugs by weighing a number of factors:

Their various actions. Each drug has complicated and sometimes opposite effects. A drug given to help a depressed person sleep may make it more difficult for him to sleep later on.

The manner of their administration. An injection of medication is likely to be more potent and quicker acting, but also less safe, than the same amount of the same medication taken by mouth. Some drugs can be regulated safely by the patient while others have only a very narrow margin between the therapeutic dose and the toxic dose and must be administered, therefore, under very close supervision. Some drugs can be taken intermittently and still achieve their effect, while others, in order to work, must be taken regularly and scrupulously for three to four weeks.

Their side effects, especially as they are likely to affect a particular patient. A drug influences many different systems of the body at once. Some of the actions are adverse. Just how adverse they are and how frequent is weighed against the beneficial effect of the drug in determining its usefulness. The actions it has on a particular person are also varied and depend on such factors as his age, sex, and general health. If he has certain physical illnesses, he cannot use certain drugs. And there are certain drugs that cannot be used with certain others or that must be taken then in reduced amounts. Alcohol may alter the effect of a drug dangerously, as may certain foods, on occasion, or other substances. For instance, patients who are taking a particular type of antidepressant drug cannot eat cheese, especially Cheddar cheese, without risking a hypertensive crisis. Neither can they drink Chianti, although most sherries, as it happens, are perfectly safe.

Consequently the complexities of prescribing are such that

7-chloro-2 methylamino-5-phenyl-3H-1.4 benzodiazepine 4 oxide hydrochloride, is never used by a physician, for obvious reasons.

no single drug regimen for the treatment of depression has emerged. The diversity of treatment, however, is not an argument for using any old medicine any old way. All decisions about the use of medication must be made carefully *by a physician*. Still, friends, family, and other collateral therapists will inevitably be involved in the drug management of the depressed person, as they are in every other aspect of his care. For one thing they will have to make sure that he takes his medicine as prescribed. Such a patient, perhaps because he is self-destructive, may very well refuse to take medicine out of a wish to punish himself, or may neglect to take it out of a sense of hopelessness. He may hoard his drugs with the intention of accumulating enough to commit suicide. In order to make sure no such thing happens, someone, usually a member of his family, should fill his prescriptions and dispense his medication to him. Even when he seems to be somewhat improved, he should not be allowed to hold his own medicine. Suicide is not uncommon at just that time when a depression seems to be lifting.

Similarly someone must take responsibility for noting any side effects that these drugs may produce in the patient, even though the significance of those effects will not be apparent.

Mr. A. was a fifty-three-year-old teacher who became very depressed after being transferred from the school in which he had taught for ten years to another school, in a slum area. His symptoms included a pervasive melancholy and the usual vegetative signs of depression, namely early morning awakening and loss of appetite and weight. He was preoccupied with what he regarded as his failings as a teacher and as a parent; he could talk of little else. He came to medical attention because of a host of physical symptoms. At the same time that he became depressed, he began to suffer constant headaches which felt to him as if a steel band had been wound tightly about his eyes and forehead. He had stomach cramps and intermittent pains in his chest. He was troubled also by belching, which came on particularly when he found himself becoming angry at his children. Among his other symptoms were a lightheaded feeling, vague blurring of vision, and an unsteadiness of gait—and nausea, shortness of breath, and trembling and tingling of his fingers.

Despite the prominence of his physical symptoms he was thought to have a relatively typical depression, and was started, therefore, on a course of treatment with one of the dibenzazepine compounds, a major class of antidepressant drugs. Within two to three weeks he improved; his mood lifted and he slept comfortably through the night. He was still bothered, however, by fatigue, dizziness, and various pains. One morning he remarked to his wife that besides his usual distress, he noticed a fluttering sensation in his chest and pain in his shoulder. These new symptoms seemed no more remarkable or ominous than any of the others that he had told his psychiatrist about over the past month and that were attributed invariably to a manifestation of his underlying depression. For just that reason Mr. A. was embarrassed to mention to him still one more minor discomfort. His wife, however, to be on the safe side, telephoned the psychiatrist and told him of this latest complaint, which, as a matter of fact, did have a special meaning. The psychiatrtist arranged immediately for Mr. A. to have a medical consultation and an electrocardiogram. This examination gave evidence of a very recent heart attack and a cardiac arrhythmia. He was hospitalized at once and his medication, which is dangerous under those particular circumstances, was stopped. By virtue of that telephone call, Mrs. A. may have saved her husband's life.

If it were true that drugs were entirely successful in curing depression, there would be no reason to be concerned with other aspects of its management; unfortunately those drugs currently in use do not work quickly, do not work forever, and sometimes do not work at all. Even when they work, the effect they achieve is not so striking that it is reasonable to talk of cure. Any one of or all of the varied symptoms of depression may last, even with treatment, for months, and even after they have faded away, they may recur periodically and unpredictably. The very depressed person, therefore, will need to be cared for in other ways. Proper treatment, in the form of supportive psychotherapy, will diminish the severity of his illness and the dangers of it—not only the danger of suicide, which is its most terrible complication, but also the dangers of invalidism and social isolation.

Someone who is emotionally ill will not be helped until he is recognized by others as being ill; yet if he is depressed, his condition may go unnoticed. He may seem simply to be upset, or in a bad mood, or perhaps physically ill, if he has physical complaints. The essential first step in treatment, therefore, is to consider seriously the unpleasant prospect that a family member or a friend may be truly depressed. Usually then the fact of his depression will become obvious. Once he is recognized as emotionally disturbed rather than simply disagreeable, it will be possible to respond to him appropriately without being disagreeable in turn. Certainly it is no help to him simply to be scolded, or goaded by being told to buck up or cheer up. He cannot be maneuvered into smiling and being happy. The depressed person should always be treated respectfully and with some deference. If he says over and over that he is a miserable and awful person, his family should not argue with him, or worse, out of exasperation, agree with him. Rather they should tell him the truth—that the awful feelings he has about himself are not due to anything bad that he has done, but are rather an outgrowth of his depression.

If a depressed person is troubled predominantly by physical symptoms, he will probably find his way to a physician on his own; but if he sees himself as guilty and as worthless, as suffering a spiritual disorder that places him beyond all redemption, then he may refuse to go for help. The family must make sure somehow that he is helped nevertheless. If it seems likely he will interpret being brought to a psychiatrist as a judgment on the part of his family that he is crazy, he may be brought initially instead to his family doctor, but in any case he must see someone competent to treat him. If necessary there are legal procedures by which a patient may be removed to a hospital against his wishes and evaluated. Usually, however, a determined family will be able on their own to convince such a person to visit a doctor.

Of course, some physicians will not knowingly become involved with a depressed patient. They may resent spending the necessary amount of time simply talking with him or his family. They may think of psychotherapy as a nonmedical pursuit and outside their training. Sometimes they are annoyed by the physical symptoms of someone who is depressed, since those symptoms seem insubstantial yet resistant to ordinary treatment. They may be annoyed by the patient himself, who is likely to be difficult and disagreeable. Finally, if they recognize a patient as seriously depressed and therefore potentially suicidal, they become concerned, naturally, that in their relatively inexperienced hands, the patient will die. And yet an ordinary clinical depression can be treated successfully by a general practitioner who is comfortable with depressed patients and willing to talk to them. Someone psychotically depressed should be, and usually is, referred on to a psychiatrist for treatment.

The family, then, find themselves at the very beginning of treatment cast in the role of liaison, or facilitator, between the patient and his primary therapist, and they will be acting in that role throughout treatment. Usually it falls to them to choose a psychiatrist. Then usually they have to encourage the patient to go to him and to keep going for a while even if he does not feel that he is being helped. They will, especially in the beginning of treatment, provide information to the psychiatrist about symptoms or problems the patient may have, perhaps at work, or within the family itself. If the patient begins to improve, or worsen, that information should be communicated also. Of course, whenever a member of the family decides that he needs to speak to the psychiatrist, he should tell the patient first and obtain his consent if possible; but if he has something important to say, he should not allow himself to be deterred by any objection the patient may make. The psychiatrist, for his part, like any therapist, may decide not to reply to questions that the family may ask of him, if he feels doing so would violate a confidence of the patient; but certainly he can listen to whatever they have to say to him.

Confidentiality in psychotherapy is never absolute, anyway, but must yield, at least, to the purpose of saving the patient's life. If the psychiatrist or any other therapist comes to believe the patient intends to kill himself, he must do something about it, if necessary by calling the police. He cannot allow himself to sit idly by and become an accomplice in a suicide. If because of the psychiatrist's intervention a suicidal patient is brought unwillingly to a hospital, invariably the patient will understand subsequently that it was in his own best interests. Their relationship will not be endangered as a result.

The primary therapist, for his part, has a number of reasons to be attentive to the family, not only for the special insight they have into the patient, but also because the patient's emotional illness may be only one part of a family illness. In treating the patient he is often involved in treating the whole family. Even at the beginning of treatment, though, before he knows them well, he must enlist their support. He may see the patient as infrequently as two or three hours a week, or less, while all the other hours of the week the patient is with his family. He may design a treatment plan, but it will fall to the family more often than not to implement that plan. Each, then, has a complementary role. They must act in concert.

Take, for example, the first clinical decision the psychiatrist has to make: whether or not to hospitalize his patient. On one hand he weighs the benefits of a particular hospital. Is it truly safe? Is the staff well trained and committed? Is there a rational treatment program? Practicing in the surrounding community, he will have come to know the answer to those questions. But on the other hand he needs to consider the alternative, namely the patient continuing to live at home. How is he to learn about circumstances at home except from the family? His patient's ability to manage is judged in the first place in large part from what they have told him.

THE HOSPITAL

There are, of course, considerations that apply generally in determining the appropriateness of hospitalization.* Someone actively suicidal has a potentially fatal condition. Under most circumstances he is better off in the hospital, first to prevent him from obtaining easy access to the usual tools of suicide, firearms or pills; and second, and perhaps more important, to communicate to him a willingness on the part of his family and the other people taking care of him to take his feelings and his illness seriously. Hospitalization is a device to underline their concern for him, their wish that he *not* kill himself.

A psychotically depressed patient cannot take care of himself very well, and so a hospital, which is organized after all around the principle of providing care, can look after him and make sure, for instance, that he eats and sleeps properly and takes his medicine. Some of the medicines he is likely to receive have side effects that require that he be observed closely,

*For a discussion of suicide and treatment and hospitalization, see pp. 88–112.

which may be accomplished readily in the hospital setting. If he needs a course of electric shock treatment, it can be given to him conveniently while he is an inpatient, as can any therapeutic or diagnostic procedure that may be indicated. Also, when a patient is removed to the hospital, both he and his family have a chance to be free for a while from the pressures of living with each other. It is a chance also for the therapist to explain to the family the proper management of the depressed patient. They should be prepared for that time when he will return to them, for it is unlikely he will return fully recovered.

The disadvantages of living in a hospital have been described at some length. It is a boring, impersonal, and demeaning existence that comes with getting up, eating, going to sleep, and doing most other things at someone else's demand, on schedule. A psychiatric patient cannot usually go out when he wants to or even make telephone calls when he wants to. He may not be permitted to read or lie down during the day. If he has been admitted to the hospital involuntarily, which happens sometimes, these petty and arbitrary constraints make it seem to him that he is living in jail. The patient is kept in the hospital also at the price of keeping him from work and from his customary habits and associations, which are usually a source of emotional support. Although sometimes hospitalization serves to communicate a concern on the part of everyone for the patient, it may seem at other times to other patients to mean a final abandonment. Once in the hospital some patients regress, apparently because they feel that in that setting they are expected to act crazy or irresponsible. However, the worst danger of hospitalization is that it allows the family and the therapist to feel they have discharged their responsibilities. They can go about their business without worrying about the patient anymore. But the hospitalization itself is never an end to treatment: it is usually only the first step.

In general, then, the severity of a depression determines the place of treatment. In favor of a patient being in the hospital are the following: a clear expression of suicidal intent; the presence of delusions or hallucinations; evidence of severe agitation or impulsive behavior; and possibly a history of drug abuse, especially alcohol or barbiturates. General considerations cannot substitute, however, for a specific knowledge of a particular patient. Someone depressed even to a psychotic degree may be treated effectively at home under certain circumstances: when the family has the resources and the determination to care for him, and when they feel comfortable working under the close and continuing supervision of a primary therapist whose judgment they trust.

In the treatment of depression, as in the treatment of all the emotional disorders mentioned in this book, the role of the primary therapist—a psychiatrist or psychologist—and that of collateral therapists—who may be anyone involved with the patient—overlap, and tend to overlap also with the role of the family. Prescribing medication may be the exclusive province of a physician, such as a psychiatrist, but supportive psychotherapy is done by everyone. The distinctions in the following paragraphs, therefore, are drawn largely for purposes of emphasis and clarity.

THE ROLE OF THE THERAPIST

The therapist must first of all see to it as best he can that his patient does not kill himself or injure himself in other ways; and those other ways are many, although the same wish to be self-destructive underlies them all. He may hurt himself physically, not only by suicide but by so-called suicide gestures, such as an overdose of aspirin, which may not kill or be intended to kill but which may provoke a peptic ulcer, or some other bodily disturbance. Slashing a wrist tentatively, even without suicidal intent, may cause damage to tendons or nerves and subsequent loss of function in the hand, or, at best, leave a scar that can never be explained away satisfactorily. At worst such a suicide gesture may go further than planned and actually cause death.

The depressed person may engage also in systematic gambling with death, by injecting himself with drugs, for example, or by driving too fast or while under the influence of alcohol. Alcohol is a theme in the lives of such people, for its use obliterates all feeling for a time; narcotics and barbiturates in high enough doses act similarly. All of these agents are in their own ways physically harmful. The depressed person may injure himself physically also by starving himself dramatically, or less dramatically, by overeating. He may become promiscuous, or overly ascetic. He may refuse to sleep, and so on. Any unhealthy or dangerous behavior may be exploited by such a person who seeks to punish himself in order to expiate his feelings of guilt. And he may injure himself in ways that are not physical. By his need to confess indiscriminately to imaginary sins he may actually convince people that he is as terrible as he thinks he is. In such a way he may ruin his reputation at work. By behaving cantankerously he may ruin his relationships with friends and with other people.

The nature of the therapeutic intervention corresponds to the particular threat. The best safeguard against suicide is the understanding on the part of the therapist, the family, and the nursing staff, if there is one, that the possibility of suicide exists in every depressed patient throughout his entire clinical course. No mechanical safeguard such as a locked room can substitute for vigilance. Those other dangers mentioned above must be countered as best they can. An attempt should be made to limit the patient's use of alcohol or other drugs. The extent to which he eats and sleeps can also be monitored. If he is behaving in such a way as to endanger his job, he should be instructed to take sick leave. The therapist must exert his influence against all these varied, maladaptive behaviors, and any others that his patient may invent. To a significant extent the therapist must order his patient's life for a while. All major decisions that can only be made by the patient, such as whether or not to marry or divorce, or change jobs, or move away, must be postponed until he is well and able to consider them rationally.

Influencing the patient to even this limited extent is not easy. The very depressed person is not in the mood to listen to anyone. He ruminates endlessly about the hopelessness and awfulness of his life, or sits silently by himself, seemingly out of reach. Sometimes all the therapist can do is sit nearby. When at last his patient does talk to him, he should listen respectfully. No response he can make is likely to be very comforting or reassuring; but he should try anyway. The act of trying itself communicates something. If he can, he should lead his patient to understand one thing at least—that he has an illness that is common rather than strange and awful, and that is treatable.

When the patient is somewhat better, which may be in a week or so, or in a number of weeks, he can be engaged more successfully in a relationship. At that point he is more likely to express openly feelings that he may not have been able to admit to previously and that may underlie his depression. Angry feelings are often prominent. Unvoiced, they seem to rankle, and worsen a depression. In the therapeutic relationship a climate is established in which the patient can be himself and express what he feels rather than what he thinks he ought to feel. For that reason he should be allowed to verbalize his feelings without contradiction, however irrational they may seem to be.

THE ROLE OF THE FAMILY

The role of the family is more often defined in terms of what they ought not to do rather than what they should do. Certainly they ought not to preempt the authority of the primary therapist. They ought not to interfere in treatment by suggesting that what the patient needs is a vacation, or vitamin injections, or home remedies of one sort or another, or some hard work for a change, or a good talking to. They ought not to scoff at or belittle the patient's worries, however ridiculous they seem to be. At the other extreme, they must not themselves become so upset at the patient's distress that they add to his guilt and distress. They should not tell the patient that he is absurd to feel guilty, for he will feel guilty nevertheless, except that he will no longer mention it to anyone. If he takes such criticism to heart, he will come to feel guilty even about feeling guilty. The family should especially not argue with him about the reasons he gives for his feelings, for they are not the real reasons. An elderly woman, for instance, may become depressed and attribute her melancholy to shame over some minor sexual transgression that took place when she was adolescent and that never entered her thoughts again during the intervening years. Whatever the real reason for her getting depressed, surely it is not that. The family should not expect the patient to be able to explain himself. Also they should not demand that he function at a level beyond his capacity. There is no point in telling him to get out in the world and work, or have some fun, if he is unable to do so. If he is given a task that is beyond him, he will fail and feel even worse. Neither, however, should they encourage him to give up entirely and take to his bed. Most important of all, they should not scold or punish him for being depressed. The person who is very depressed is not crying, complaining, clinging, and behaving helplessly, out of spite, but because he cannot help it. Whatever he may say to the contrary, his condition is not self-inflicted. He is not suffering because he has done something wrong but because he has an illness, which although less tangible than a heart attack, is no less real and strikes no less forcibly.

However, the members of his family do have a positive role to play, for they are the principal actors in his life. Very little that he experiences or accomplishes takes place entirely out of their view, and whatever he has become, the person that he is, is to an extent a response to them. At times of crisis they have the most influence over him, and they are his chief resource. He is a difficult person to help, though, often irascible and stubborn; and so they must be patient with him and persistent in their determination to care for him. They cannot afford to become angry and throw up their hands in despair. If he is depressed and withdrawn and seemingly out of reach, he may still appreciate on some level those ordinary things that people do for each other. Even wanting to withdraw, he may want someone to come after him. The family, then, should see to it that the patient is not isolated. He should be treated with courtesy and forbearance and included in family planning as if he were expected to recover and remain among them rather than fade away. No one should venture to sell his car while he is in the hospital, or give up his apartment. Nor should he be allowed to make such decisions while he is acutely depressed. When he is at home, however irritable he may be, he should not be sequestered in a room away from his children and the rest of his family and the everyday business of the household.

In all matters concerning the plans for his treatment, he should be informed at once. If it is decided he must be in a hospital, he should not be brought there under some pretext, but rather with a clear understanding of the reasons for his hospitalization. He should be told how long he is expected to remain; once he is there, his family should communicate with him as closely as circumstances allow—by personal visit, telephone, and even letter. Living in a hospital is otherwise a very lonely experience. The family must not, however, out of their sympathy with the patient, give in to any demands he may make to be removed from the hospital prematurely and against medical advice. In general throughout this period of treatment they should encourage him to follow strictly the advice of his doctor.

The important issues, the patient should be reminded, are not in the irrevocable past, or in the unknowable future, but in the present. He must consider his days one at a time and tend to his daily needs, eating and dressing himself properly and being with other people at least some of the time. Often he will do these simple things for his family's sake. The application of these simple principles of nursing care sometimes makes the difference between an illness that comes and goes like any other illness, and an illness so disruptive of life that it predisposes to invalidism and leaves behind it a permanent mark on the individual and his family.

A fifty-year-old man was significantly depressed, but not to such a degree that he needed to be in a hospital. He was treated instead as an outpatient. He was feeling badly enough, however, to stay home from work. He spent the days sitting in his room staring into space. He was sullen and irritable, which was a marked change of his personality, since he was usually effusive. In fact, he was usually so friendly and jolly that he was assigned the role of Santa Claus every Christmas; he found the role so congenial that he not infrequently dressed up in his Santa Claus suit during Easter.

Consequently his family felt terrible seeing him so out of sorts. His wife came to him frequently with sandwiches or soup or something else for him to eat, only to be turned away. His friends came by to play cards, but he would not come out of his room even to greet them. Because he enjoyed sports, his sons bought tickets for a professional basketball game and when he would not go willingly with them, they attempted to remove him to the stadium bodily, with the result that he tried to punch one of them, missed, and fell over, spraining his ankle. He was glad he couldn't walk, he announced to his doctor that night, for maybe finally his family would leave him alone. A month later, though, when he was better, he confided that even at those times when his family badgered him the most with their constant attention, they comforted him, for he said to himself that he could not be too awful a person if they were willing to try so hard to be nice to him.

Certainly it is possible to go too far, as this family plainly did, in attempting to command the patient's interest. Attending a sporting event or some other entertainment is not by itself therapeutic and is not worth fighting over. Besides, everyone in the world needs to be left alone sometimes, and a depressed person needs those moments no less than everyone else. But his family should err on the side of too much involvement with him rather than too little, for he is better off engaged too vigorously than neglected and left alone.

THE PERIOD OF AFTERCARE

The length of a psychotic depression is described variously in the psychiatric literature as lasting without treatment from nine months to a year and a half, or two years. Without treatment a minority of cases are said to become chronic and never improve. But, of course, there are effective treatments for depression and there have been for many years, so that these figures do not represent anyone's current experience. A severe depression can be expected to last with current methods of treatment only a matter of weeks or months, at least in the great majority of cases. But those weeks and months must be regarded only as prelude to a longer period in which the patient must come to terms with the meaning of his illness.

A depression is an unpleasant pause in the precipitous course of life. Suddenly the individual sees himself, his routine occupations, his ambitions, his relationships with others, as without value. Even when that perception has faded after a while, he cannot then settle himself comfortably into his previous existence as if he had never been depressed. Lingering is a more precarious sense of himself. And the depressed state has a tendency to recur. Preventing such a recurrence is the principal goal of treatment during this period after the resolution of the acute depression. To that purpose, the primary therapist is careful not to stop treatment prematurely. He allows the patient to become independent of him slowly, continuing to see him occasionally for months in order to watch for the return of symptoms. If the patient is neurotic, which is frequently but not invariably the case, the therapist may encourage him to enter into insight psychotherapy, which follows logically out of the relationship they have already established.

At this point the patient requires less supervision from his family and the other people who care about him. All they can do now is facilitate, perhaps, that which he must do really on his own. He must examine the kind of person he is. If he has spent his life trying to satisfy other people's expectations, he must set out now to be different, to be himself. Those who are subject to depression live sometimes by a stultifying ethic: that they cannot be angry at anyone, for then they will be unloved; that they cannot enjoy themselves frivolously, for then they will be unworthy; that they cannot be spontaneous or alive or original, for then they will be unacceptable to everyone else. Such a way of life is unworkable and predisposes to depression. Unfortunately such traits of character are the bedrock of personality and do not readily change. Nevertheless, the self-conscious self-doubting that is the unpleasant aftermath of an acute depression can be turned to special advantage as an opportunity to focus the patient's attention meaningfully upon himself. It is a time when change is possible.

The patient's family must recognize his need to be different. Too often they prefer him the way he used to be: compliant, undemanding if not uncomplaining, inhibited, and unobtrusive. If he is to grow at all, they must make room for him. If he is going to assert himself, it will be at their expense every once in a while. Still, in the long run they will prefer to live with someone who is spontaneous and full of life rather than someone who is depressed intermittently and withdrawn a considerable part of the time. In general every patient recovering from a depression should be encouraged to do certain things.

He should first of all consider how he wants to spend his life. If his goals are unreasonable, he should modify them or think of something else to strive for. Some of the ambitions people have are not only out of reach but are not worth reaching for in the first place: to be liked by everyone, to be sexually attractive to everyone, to be worshiped by one's children, to outshine all of one's colleagues, or to be young forever.

If he has become depressed because he has suffered a special loss, such as the death of a spouse, he must find some sort of replacement, perhaps one single person, but if not, then friends. Everyone must learn to be alone sometimes without feeling empty or abandoned, but no one can be entirely alone. If that loss is a job, perhaps through retirement, he must find something else worth doing. Work, at any age, is better than a hobby, and a hobby is better than watching television or doing nothing at all. Best of all is work that is useful and satisfying.

The person who has been depressed should be encouraged to express himself openly, particularly to talk about and work through those ideas that he may have communicated impulsively during the acute phase of his illness. Such ideas, however irrational, ought not to be dismissed as simply one more manifestation of a pathological state of mind. Even if it is true that they would never have been voiced had he not been distraught, they are his ideas nevertheless and an expression of deep-seated feelings. A woman who reports when she is depressed that she has been a terrible mother must have had doubts at other times about her relationship with her children. There is opportunity during this emotional lull after the storm for the patient to come to terms with such feelings and explore ways of being different.

DEPRESSION IN CHILDHOOD AND ADOLESCENCE

The previous discussion has made the assumption for didactic purposes that all depressed people resemble each other; in many ways they do, especially when that depression is of psychotic degree. But in many other ways they do not. A depression may show itself simply in a failure to live successfully, to accomplish age-appropriate tasks. A child who is depressed may not complain of feeling sad, but rather of not getting along with his friends or not wanting to go to school. He may regress to behavior seemingly outgrown previously, such as bed-wetting, or show a change in bowel habits, such as soiling or constipation. These symptoms may appear by themselves or together with more blatant disturbances of mood. Similarly, if the task of adolescence is to separate emotionally from parents and become self-reliant, a depressed adolescent may show as his principal symptom the wish to stay home by himself. He loses interest in school and in work, and avoids his friends. Or he may run away in an attempt to become independent all at once. The inclination to injure oneself may show itself at this age in antisocial behavior such as stealing, promiscuity, or the abuse of drugs and alcohol. Each of these behavior problems may require treatment apart from the underlying depression that causes them. Avoidance of school, for instance, sometimes called a school phobia, will become chronic if not treated promptly, usually in part by bringing the child or adolescent to school despite his fears. If he becomes fixed in the habit of remaining at home, his entire subsequent experience with school will be adversely affected. School counselors can be particularly helpful during the slow transition from school to home. For another example, promiscuity, which may grow out of the contempt a depressed adolescent feels for himself or herself, may lessen considerably simply if the young person can discuss it with a sympathetic, nonjudgmental person. To an extent, talking about a sexual impulse, or any other kind of impulse, can substitute for the impulsive act. Shoplifting, when it is impulsive, often goes away in the beginnings of therapy. Either symptom unattended can set a pattern of behavior that continues into adult life long after the resolution of the depression that first provoked it.

The depression that appears in childhood and adolescence is more variable than that of adulthood, both in its symptoms and its course. The younger the person, the less likely it is that medication will work or be considered appropriate. An unhappy child is often the barometer of an unhappy family, and often the only treatment that really helps is family therapy. The adolescent represents a special problem, both to his family and to anyone acting as therapist. Like anyone who is depressed, he is sullen, irritable, and withdrawn. He may seem to his parents to be lazy and rebellious rather than depressed, unwilling to work rather than unable. He sees them, of course, as unsympathetic. A therapist has to spend considerable time mediating between them. Under those circumstances he may have trouble winning the patient's confidence. The adolescent may insist on seeing him as an agent of his parents or as some other authority figure, and consequently wrangle with him unceasingly. The therapist must be careful not to respond by scolding. He should listen respectfully, and go out of his way not to patronize his patient by putting on a pose of being an adolescent himself, for example, by speaking in the vernacular of adolescence. Such a mask is transparent.

He must be straightforward, and, of course, he must be the sort of person who can tolerate the conflicts and the contradictions—and the turmoil—of adolescence.

ADULT AND INVOLUTIONAL DEPRESSION

Life is characterized by struggle, and inevitably from time to time that struggle is unsuccessful; in the wake of failure may come depression.

The failures of work may not be recognizable as such to others, for they may represent only the inability of the individual to live up to his own goals and standards. At the age of thirty one can no longer expect, as an adolescent would, to master every occupation and accomplish every purpose; for some people even such an inevitable failure is a keenly felt disappointment. At the age of forty there looms up the possibility that even a single occupation may not be mastered. And at the age of fifty most people have to confront the clear realization that they will never reach their occupational goals; for those few who have reached them, some find that the achievement has not been worth the effort. They may have struggled for acceptance and recognition and found instead only the resentment of other people. Some who struggle just as hard find themselves at that age, through no fault of their own, without a job at all—a failure in everyone's eyes.

There is no convenient remedy for a failure at work except a subsequent success; but the individual must be able to recognize success. He must measure himself by a more enlightened standard than simply by his rank within a company or by how much money he makes. He should ask himself if he has achieved something worthwhile, and if he has tried his best; and if he has enjoyed himself. If not, then he must begin to work at something else, to try again. Still, the opportunity to succeed at work, particularly meaningful work, is not afforded everyone. Some people fail. Such a person can be helped then only by being convinced that he is valuable still by the standards of those people who love him.

People fail at marriage. These failures are as varied as all the possible combinations of two people; but the outcome typically is divorce. Almost half of all marriages terminate in divorce, and, no doubt, some portion of the others are so unhappy they too ought to have been brought to an end. The process of breaking apart is so painful, however, and difficult, financially and otherwise, that it is never entered into until the couple is unequivocally miserable. By that time they seem to hate each other. In most states the laws that regulate divorce set the couple more than ever against each other and then, after the divorce is granted, somehow manage to leave each of them at a disadvantage with respect to the other. The bitterness of a typical divorce proceeding and the loneliness that follows bring with them, not infrequently, an overt clinical depression. Being alone, by itself, predisposes to depression. And so the divorced, the widowed, and all those others who have never married in the first place are vulnerable.

If someone who is divorced, or for that matter widowed, is not to become depressed, he must find new direction to his life. He must plan to occupy himself usefully, and particularly to be with people, for otherwise even a few empty days will make his life seem desolate. Suicide sometimes occurs in the period immediately before or after a divorce; yet if this moment of crisis can be weathered, a successful life can be reconstructed. The help of other family members and friends is vital at such a time.

Perhaps the difficulties of living as an adult become most obvious during the involutional period, which is considered usually to be in the late forties or fifties, but which is really not a particular age but rather a time of particular stresses. These include:

The loss of children, who have grown up and moved away.

The loss of sexual attractiveness.

The loss of the vitality of youth and the corresponding emergence, one after the other, of the physical evidences of aging, such as the menopause.

And finally, the loss of self-esteem that comes from having reached a place in work where no further advance is possible.

Many people will have to face the additional strains of poverty, of the death of friends and of parents, and of illness. Certain illnesses are especially traumatic and well-known for causing depression, among them, for example, a heart attack in a man or mutilative surgery in a woman such as a hysterectomy or the removal of a breast.

No one can live through this age of life without experiencing some of these losses, and no one does so with complete equanimity. Some people, however, find it especially hard to adjust. A man who has dedicated himself to work is especially vulnerable to losing his job, or to even a change of job. Similarly, there are men whose respect for themselves has always rested on their athletic or sexual prowess; as these abilities inevitably decline, the value they put on themselves drops correspondingly. Such men have counterparts in the woman who has committed her life to her children and suddenly finds that they no longer need her, and in the other woman who has made her way through life by flirting and who judges her worth by the number of men who court and admire her. A middle-aged woman who is girlish becomes an object of ridicule rather than admiration.

These people suffer from having lived narrow lives, and they can help themselves only by learning to be different. They have to learn a new purpose, a new reason for living. At least a little, they have to abandon their former selves. Yet some people are so set in the ways they have always followed that they cannot or will not change. They prefer to be themselves rather than to be happy.

SENILITY AND DEPRESSION IN THE AGED

As men and women grow older, eventually, inevitably, they grow old. To them the transition is subtle and impalpable. They are still, it seems to them, the people they always were. They are still the sum of their past lives: their habits, attitudes, and longings; their occupations and their pastimes; the occasional extraordinary things that have happened to them, and also the ordinary things, the simple business of all their days. They remember themselves throughout all of those days. They think now more or less the same thoughts they thought then, and feel the same feelings. They recognize in the mirror the same face, which doesn't seem to have changed since they were children, except in some small, unimportant ways. They are still somewhere inside them their young selves. And yet there is a time when they know they are old. They have learned it from other people, that they are old and are expected, therefore, to behave in certain ways, as an old person behaves. That role is defined by the commonly held ideas of a society. It is a cultural role and though not precise or explicit, it has a powerful influence on people. From the time they are called old, the lives of these men and women will depend on how well they can adjust to or, more often, resist the constraints of that role; and that, in turn, is a function of character.

Considering the way old people are treated, it is evident that society makes three judgments about them:

Because of their diminished mental capacity, and their old-fashioned ideas—they know nothing.

Since they are infirm and feeble—they can do nothing.

And, finally, because they are isolated and quiet—they want nothing.

So they are forced to retire from work, and from life, and

they subside finally into a soft chair to be hypnotized by a television set.

This glib and outrageous stereotype bears no relation to the actual circumstances of old age, but is a careless rationalization to justify the neglect and disregard of society. The aged are put to one side because they are ugly, because they remind people of what someday they will become. Such usage of the aged must change. They are not being served properly. It is terrible that so universal and natural a condition as being old should be repugnant to everyone.

Growing old is at any event a depressing experience. Besides those problems of the involutional period, many of which seem to continue into old age, there are new and devastating problems. The person who is old may have suffered difficulties at work in the past, but these culminate finally in his having no work at all. So there is an end to competition and struggle, but also an end to the satisfaction of accomplishing something that society values sufficiently high to reward with money. Someone who has measured himself by his income suddenly finds that he is worthless.

Sexual attractiveness and sexual behavior itself, which may have ebbed during the involutional period, recede still further. Although there is no age so advanced that a sexual life is automatically precluded, the older a person is, the less likely he is, statistically, to engage in sex. One reason is that he may be ill. Another important reason is the increasing likelihood as time goes on that he will be alone and without an opportunity for sex.

There is a reality, therefore, to growing old that will always apply no matter what the values of the society. Whoever lives long enough must, without fail, suffer two principal losses: the loss of the important people in his life and the loss of the proper functioning of his body. If he is lucky, neither loss is catastrophic; but still they are real and unavoidable. Any man who lives long enough will see his wife die, and brothers and sisters and friends, even sometimes his children. The loss of a child in particular is always felt keenly, for it is abnormal somehow—a violation of the natural order of things, even when the child is an adult. So, in the end, there is loneliness. There must be new people entering into these old lives, for utter loneliness is unbearable.

The loss of physical functioning follows no consistent pattern. It is the result of a wide range of illnesses, no single one of which is inevitable but which in sum cannot be avoided altogether. These illnesses tend to affect certain organ systems, such as the special senses. For instance vision is attacked by vascular and metabolic disorders, cataracts, and a host of other conditions. Consequently, as people age, an increasing proportion have poor eyesight, and significant numbers become blind. This cruel handicap is awful for anyone but falls particularly hard on those who are old and already infirm. Similarly, old people become deaf. They sit in a corner of the room not hearing anyone and perhaps after a while not wanting to hear anyone. And old people lose their taste and smell and, along the way, their interest in food. If they become depressed and further lose their appetite, they become malnourished and still more infirm.

Therefore the aged need prompt and adequate medical care so that small illnesses do not become large and incapacitating. They must have proper-fitting dentures and eyeglasses or hearing aids, if those are required. They should have an adequate diet and proper clothing. Medicines should be available to them when needed.

Another important physical limitation is the lack of mobility that people suffer increasingly as they get older. Arthritis makes the act of walking painful, while diseases of the heart and lungs make it exhausting. Some find it impossible to climb stairs, and there are some who live out their lives in a wheelchair. Medical attention can alleviate these conditions too. But as a group the aged lack mobility in a more profound sense.

Usually because they cannot drive, they travel only at the convenience of their families or they depend on public transportation. Sometimes they are afraid of going out at all because they might fall and hurt themselves or be attacked by someone. After a while the real dangers of the city fuse with imaginary ones and the world becomes a place of menace—and they have nowhere to go.

These varied handicaps, and all the others to which man is liable, all serve to constrict the lives of the aged, to undermine their skills and limit their pleasure. A woman may not sew; a man may not read the paper. The appreciation of music is diminished or lost. The pace of life falters and drifts into tedium.

And there is the fact of chronic illness itself, for almost all the diseases of man strike most forcibly at this time of life. Anyone who has been sick for a little while can imagine how it is to be sick forever, feeling miserable and irritable all the time, preoccupied with the petty business of coughing or urinating or moving one's bowels, and enduring the exasperation of nurses and family. Those who are old become ill and their bodies pain them and demean them. They become sordid to themselves.

Still, the most terrible disabilities of all are those of the mind. The mechanism of speech may be impaired by a stroke or other disorders of the brain. There may even be a disorganization of the ability to use and comprehend language itself. This condition, which is called aphasia, transports the individual suddenly to a strange and dreadful country where everyone speaks a foreign language and even the names of familiar objects are unknown to him. And then there is senility, the abhorred atrophy of the personality which is associated in the minds of many people with the process of aging itself.

Senility, or senile dementia, is a mental condition that is

supposed to result from irreversible vascular or degenerative diseases of the brain; but actually the causes are social and psychological as well. Indeed the symptoms of the old person who is senile and the old person who is depressed are often the same. And both conditions are responsive to some extent to psychological treatment. The signs of senility are familiar: forgetfulness, particularly for recent events; emotional lability or irritability; confusion; disorientation; an inability to concentrate; and a deterioration of the ability to think abstractly.

These deficiencies, which may develop very slowly, result in behavior that is socially maladroit. The senile person may wander away from his home and become lost. He may not recognize friends or even children. He may not dress properly or attend to personal hygiene. He may take clothing or other articles that belong to other people out of the mistaken belief that they are his. He may be rude or impulsive or approach strangers with sexual propositions. Unpleasant traits of his personality, which may have been mere foibles previously, become exaggerated to the point where even his family cannot put up with him—perhaps his family least of all. The senile individual may become paranoid, since he has trouble understanding the world; but especially, he may become depressed. He retreats into himself. It even seems possible at this age for a person simply to lie down and die, if death is what he wishes.

Senility and depression are related to each other. The beginnings of forgetfulness in a schoolteacher, for instance, are so painful that a clinical depression may ensue. And similarly a depression may worsen the irritability and eccentricity and even the forgetfulness that characterize senility. Both conditions are in a way part of each other. Unfortunately any elderly person who is emotionally disturbed is likely to be called senile and therefore ignored out of the presumption that such a condition is untreatable. Yet such patients, sometimes even after being put away in an institution for years, will respond to persistent efforts to draw them out, to become involved with them as human beings. When they become less isolated, their memory improves, as does all of their intellectual functioning. They begin to find their way about without getting lost. Their mood improves. They seem to grow younger. It is not only the physical changes in the brain that cause senility but also the isolation of old age and particularly that of institutional life.

A reasonable treatment regimen for senility, either at home or in an institution, offers the individual two opportunities: to engage in activities that are interesting and useful, and to be with other people. And the same regimen is fundamental to the treatment of the elderly person who is depressed. The best activities are those that the individual has always enjoyed; the closer they resemble work, the better. A mechanic can still fix a car even if his memory is beginning to falter. A cook can still cook. If they are depressed, they can still do these things; or at least they should be encouraged to try. Accomplishing useful work, even if it is unpaid, is unmistakable evidence of being worthwhile. The people with whom the elderly should associate should be active and alive, although all too often they are not. An old person is likely for no special reason to be consigned to a nursing home and surrounded there by people who are moribund or themselves senile.

An effective program of treatment for the senile patient will also include proper amounts of exercise, a comfortable and varied number of activities, and familiar surroundings in which he may feel secure. Since he may wake up at night, a light should be kept on in his room to lessen the chance of his becoming confused. Psychotherapy, individually or in groups, is a help in discouraging objectionable behavior and in further involving the senile patient with other people. The extent of such relationships, however, is limited usually by the defect of his memory, which may persist to a greater or lesser degree despite treatment, depending on the degree of underlying organic pathology.

All therapeutic measures may reflect, of course, a reasonable assessment of what the patient can do, and he should not be pressed beyond the limit of those abilities. Indeed, there is a point beyond which his family should not be pressed to go in treating him. For instance, if he endangers the household by smoking carelessly in bed, or if he exposes himself to his grandchildren, he must be admitted into a nursing home. Any physician that does not make that recommendation is doing a disservice to the patient and to his family. Sometimes the only way a senile patient can be maintained at home is at the sacrifice of everyone else, and such a burden is unfair.

Poverty is the final complication of these conditions. Money becomes very important when there is too little of it. It buys respect and independence, both of which the aged find otherwise in short supply, for all the reasons that are given above. And there are many who cannot afford even food and clothing.

Depression occurs at every age, often causing age-specific disturbances of behavior. Because of the variety of its symptoms, it may be confused also with a number of other emotional disorders, such as anxiety states, or with physical disorders. For that reason physicians, and families of patients too, must suspect that any complaint of a patient, physical or otherwise, may be a mask for a clinical depression. Such a patient will not recover if those symptoms become the focus of attention and the underlying depression is neglected. Treatment must vary flexibly to correspond with the various problems of a particular patient. Although depression may be an illness, the problems that grow out of it are practical and exist in every aspect of living. A rational plan must be devised to cope with these difficulties as they appear. Treatment is made up not only of pills and other prescriptions, but of a special climate of feeling. The person who is depressed must be taken care of by people who themselves find meaning in life and find it worth living.

7 MANIA

IF a clinical depression is an exaggeration of the ordinary feelings of sadness and discontent that people feel from time to time, then at the other pole there is a grotesque exaggeration of the equally prosaic feelings of gaiety and joy; that condition is mania. How nice it would be if some people were given to joyous moods for no particular reason just as some others are given to moods of melancholy; indeed it seems at first glance that there are such people, and that, as a matter of fact, they are some of the same people who at other times become sad. Unfortunately, however, their moods of exhilaration turn out to be not so much joyful as frantic—not happy really but rather excited and agitated. The manic person is the personification of the antic spirit, boisterous and clownish and full of humor, but also he is easily frustrated and angered, sometimes enraged. Strangely there are also times—even when he is at his merriest—when he seems to be struggling against a feeling of depression. Between moments of exuberance, his face may shrink into an expression of somber preoccupation or distress. Sometimes the extremes of his mood lead into each other and within hours he may descend from the most sublime exaltation to an anguished despair. However, if one single state of mind summarizes the manic condition, it is neither that of gaiety nor depression but of excitement.

It is rare for an individual to have episodes of mania without at other times having episodes of depression; for that reason this condition is called manic-depressive illness or, alternatively, manic-depressive psychosis, since the disturbances of mood it causes are frequently of psychotic degree. Sometimes, however, a manic episode may appear as a less severe disturbance marked only by a relative euphoria and a relative excitement, and such a state is called hypomania. At the other extreme of mania, which is really the furthest extension of an already extreme condition, there is hyperacute delirious mania, a rare confusional state which may be fatal. Since these conditions merge into each other, there is little reason to distinguish them carefully. The distinction between hypomania and ordinary good spirits is more important but is drawn with the same difficulty psychiatrists have in general distinguishing disordered behavior from that which is normal. Ordinarily diagnosis in psychiatry has little significance. Most illnesses are defined vaguely by symptom rather than etiology, and treatment depends on the nature of those symptoms rather than on their cause. Manic-depressive illness is an exception, however. During the last few years, a drug, lithium carbonate, has been found to be effective at ameliorating and preventing attacks of mania and even attacks of depression when they occur in someone who has a history of manic episodes. It is important to know, therefore, whether someone is really manic-depressive, or whether he has some other condition with which that illness might be confused. Unfortunately there is no laboratory test or any other sure indicator of mania. The diagnosis is made still by the combination of the patient's family history, the previous course of his illness, and his current clinical presentation. The following is an account of a manic episode in a man whose life, however remarkable it seems, demonstrated no special problems that did not grow out of the usual symptoms of a manic-depressive illness; he can be regarded, therefore, as typical of that condition.

At the age of forty Mr. T. was admitted to a psychiatric hospital against his wishes, partly in response to his having purchased a thirty-foot sloop for the purpose, he said, of finding a sea passage between the Hudson River and the Mississippi. He had applied to the National Institute of Mental Health for financial support for this project on the grounds that his mental health would be better served by a vacation than by another stay in a mental hospital.

He was brought in handcuffs into the hospital examining room, singing raucously and from time to time breaking into a little dance. He was dressed rakishly. He wore a red blazer, scarlet slacks, and a red shirt which was, however, soiled and wrinkled as if he had worn it for a number of days. He wore sunglasses. His hair was uncombed, and he was sweating in response, obviously, to his exertions, for he was in continual restless movement. Throughout the interview he sat, then stood, then danced a little, then sat down again. His mood was expansive. He said that he felt marvelously well, and he began to sing an aria from Wagner, not exactly as Wagner wrote it, he admitted, but as Wagner would have written it had he had "more style." Then he launched into an account of his theories of music and from there into a discussion of a new religion that he had founded and that was based on the mysteries of a five-note scale that, he said, secretly underlay all liturgical music. When the interviewer agreed that these were tantalizing ideas, Mr. T. congratulated him on his judgment. "You're a good thinker for a headshrinker," he announced and burst into laughter. He offered to endow a university in the interviewer's name. Later on, however, when the interviewer tentatively disagreed with Mr. T.'s ideas for a world government based on sexual freedom, Mr. T. called him "a stinker of a headshrinker." He became angry. He complained about the books on the interviewer's desk, saying that they revealed a "small mind," and he knocked one of them to the floor. He refused to speak further with anyone of such little intellect, but then apparently could not remain silent. He spoke animatedly about his plans to run for public office and to reform the judiciary, and he mentioned that he had already communicated with the President in support of these ideas. Occasionally he commented derisively about his in-laws or about the dour policeman who stood by his side. He expounded on many random subjects and, as if to drive home the point, quoted from the Lewis Carroll poem "The Walrus and the Carpenter" of it being time " 'To talk of many things:/Of shoes—and ships—and sealing-wax—/Of cabbages—and kings—.' "

A review of Mr. T's medical records made at this time revealed that he had been admitted to the psychiatric hospital on four previous occasions, three of those times with the diagnosis of depression and the fourth with the diagnosis of mania. His mother and his sister had been admitted to the same hospital at one time or another, each with the diagnosis of manic-depressive illness.

Mr. T. spent the next few days after his admission taking charge of the psychiatric ward on which he had been placed. He devised and posted a schedule of recommended activities, which included regular exercises, outings in the park, and sexual play. When the staff refused to implement this program, he organized a grievance committee and was able to attract to it the support of a number of other patients. Otherwise he behaved much as he had on his initial interview. He was filled with energy. He talked and walked constantly and had little need, he said, for food or sleep. Indeed, he seemed not to sleep at all. Usually he was in a splendid humor, but when contradicted he would fly into a rage. On rare occasions he seemed to be frightened by the extravagance of his own behavior, but the next minute he was off again—ordering the staff about; offering himself sexually to the women, intruding into the conversations of other people and pointing out to them the errors of their judgment, at the same time entertaining and annoying everyone, joking, teasing, rhyming, punning, and singing.

This kaleidoscope of motion and noise is the manic. There are perhaps three cardinal features of his condition, each of which Mr. T. illustrated well:

1. An exaggeration of mood with sudden shifts back and forth from elation, which is the dominant mood, to anger. When a manic is euphoric, he is given over to great optimism and confidence. He is grandiose. No achievement is beyond him. He is so certain of his abilities, and enthusiastic, that he is convincing to others, and he may be able to enlist others in the most fantastic schemes. Since the manic is not infrequently a talented person, some of these projects come to fruition and may turn out to be worthwhile. Most, however, certainly do not.

A woman who was manic spent thousands of dollars in a single week on clothes in order to further an imaginary career on the stage. Also, it was her habit when ill to stay up all night writing novels. A manic gentleman, who happened to be in the hospital at the same time, gave out checks in the amount of one million dollars each to acquaintances as a token of affection or on occasion to strangers as a gratuity. It was hard to know whether he really believed he had a fabulous fortune as he claimed or whether he was making fun of everyone.

2. A defect of thinking caused by rapid shifts of attention and evidenced by greatly accelerated speech. The manic may start talking about his plans for building an extra room onto

his house and proceed to talk in rapid succession about the size of the Pentagon, then about troop movements in Europe, then about his experience in the army, and so on. Left to ramble on, he may return at some point to the extra room on his house, or he may not. He may discourse in ever wider circles indefinitely.

Such a "flight of ideas" usually has a connecting thread, however fragile, and is distinguished theoretically from the more fragmented "loosening of associations" that characterizes schizophrenic thought. In practice, however, the clinician is likely to make a judgment on other grounds about the patient's diagnosis and then describe the patient's thinking in terms of "flight of ideas" if he thinks the patient is manic and in terms of "loosening of associations" if he thinks he is schizophrenic.

3. An extraordinary increase in physical activity. The manic is in constant movement. He seems to resent the prospect of sitting still for a moment, or worse, going to sleep. Although he becomes fatigued like everyone else, he will not admit to it. The more tired he becomes, the more driven he is to restless, impulsive, and sometimes aggressive behavior. He has a need, apparently, to escape from his feelings into action—or perhaps his feelings are so strong that he is impelled by them into action.

Because the manic is impulse-ridden, he violates social conventions and becomes obnoxious to other people. He says whatever he feels like saying. He is a busybody. Angry feelings go unrestrained so that he is always at the center of some contention. Sexual impulses may intrude also so that a woman may be seductive and hostile at the same time; or such impulses may find immediate expression in careless promiscuity, with the result that venereal diseases and unwanted pregnancies are not uncommon complications. Dominating all the behavior of the manic, however, sexual or otherwise, is his constant excitement and hyperactivity.

A condition resembling mania can occur transiently as part of a reaction to certain drugs such as the amphetamines, as part of a stress reaction such as may occur on the battlefield, or, indeed, as part of a number of other severe emotional disturbances; but mania that lasts for a number of days or longer is usually regarded as a manifestation of a manic-depressive illness.

THE CLINICAL COURSE

The beginnings of a manic-depressive illness can be said to be in previous generations, for it is a genetic disease. At least in certain families the mode of transmission is through a sex-linked dominant gene, so that a man with this illness will have had a mother who was also manic-depressive, and will in turn communicate the disease to all of his daughters. But it turns out that there are many who should be manic-depressive who are not. It may be that this illness is really a group of illnesses transmitted by different genetic routes. What is transmitted, in any case, is only a vulnerability to an attack. The expression of a gene in an affected individual may depend on, among other things, the emotional climate in which that person lives, on other aspects of his health, in some subtle way on his upbringing, or even on his diet. The genetic hypothesis may explain the clustering of manic-depressive patients in certain families and, in general, why twice as many women are affected as men, but it will not allow the certain prediction of which children will have attacks of the disease when they are grown. Neither can it predict which individuals, having once developed a psychotic episode, will then relapse again in the future and which others will instead be well from that time on. Besides the genetic hypothesis there are psychological theories that explain manic-depressive illness in terms of events in early childhood and in terms of unconscious impulses and needs; but these too have little predictive value and do not generate a rationale for a specific treatment.

Manic-depressive illness is defined not only by the severe extremes of mood that it causes but by its tendency to remission and recurrence. The great majority of patients who have had a manic episode will have either a second such episode at some later point in their lives, or at some point will become psychotically depressed. The first manic episode rarely occurs before late adolescence and may not occur until the twenties or thirties or even later. Prior to that first episode there is little to mark the individual who will someday become manic-depressive.

The attack itself may last untreated anywhere from a few days to many years, although a period of a few months is typical. It may develop slowly or very suddenly. Sometimes the most profound mania develops within a few hours out of a depression of equal severity. For that reason mania has sometimes been thought of as a psychological defense against the terrible pain of a depression. Usually after an acute psychotic episode subsides, the individual returns to a normal level of functioning. Even after a number of attacks of mania and depression the manic-depressive is likely during those periods between attacks to show little evidence of deterioration of personality or of his abilities, and in this respect differs markedly from the schizophrenic, who becomes wasted away emotionally after recurrent periods of psychosis. As may be readily imagined, however, even a single manic attack is seriously disruptive of life, and the threat of more to come looms ominously from then on.

TREATMENT

A manic attack is usually best treated in the hospital, where some check can be applied to the patient's egregious behavior.

If he is frankly psychotic, in other words raving, he will be brought to a hospital usually through one contrivance or another, even against his wishes. But if he is not quite so ill, he may not fulfill those special requirements by which he can be hospitalized involuntarily. He is not dangerous to himself in the sense of being suicidal, at least he will not admit to such ideas. On the contrary, by his account the world is all sunshine and roses. Nor does he give evidence of being dangerous to other people. He may be argumentative and annoying, but he is not likely to harm anyone. There may, therefore, be no way of forcing him into any form of treatment. In some states if two physicians certify that, although not dangerous, the patient is unambiguously sick and in need of inpatient psychiatric care, he can be removed against his will to the hospital. Frequently, though, the first evidence of a developing manic attack is only the tendency to go without sleep and perhaps a subtle shift of mood recognized only by his family. Their experience with him during previous manic episodes and their close day-to-day contact with him give them a special insight into his condition. By anyone else's standard he may seem normal. In such a hypomanic state he may seem to be simply energetic rather than agitated. Someone talking to him may find him lively and cheerful rather than ecstatic or in some other grossly exaggerated mood. He may feel good, even very good, and not recognize himself as being sick at all; because he believes in himself, he is convincing to other people.

And yet even if he is not suicidal, he may be harmful to himself in other ways. In his blind enthusiasm and inability to take note of real obstacles, he becomes irresponsible. He is likely to enter into risky financial ventures that have the potential to ruin him. For this reason he may be declared legally incompetent to handle his own affairs at the same time that he is not quite sick enough to be committed involuntarily to a hospital! These legal distinctions tend to blur in the face of a rapidly changing clinical picture. Someone not quite sick enough to hospitalize today may be blatantly psychotic tomorrow.

In favor of hospitalizing a manic patient immediately are the following:

1. An inability on his part to recognize that he is ill. Someone who thinks he is managing terrifically well will not be inclined to cooperate in outpatient psychotherapy.

2. Reckless behavior. If someone impulsively enters into unsuitable sexual liaisons, or into poorly thought out business ventures, or if he spends large sums of money indiscriminately, then he needs to be protected against himself. Otherwise he may dissipate a lifetime's savings. Usually these adventures can be stopped effectively only by bringing him into a hospital. Similarly he should be hospitalized if he is behaving in such obtrusive and self-indulgent ways that he may otherwise permanently damage his career and his friendships with other people.

3. A deteriorating relationship with his family. The manic is exceedingly trying. He exhausts the people around him. Just as some families are better able than others to tolerate a hyperactive child, some families are better than others at putting up with the manic; but in the final analysis there is a point beyond which no family should be expected to go. Before everyone is made miserable, he should be hospitalized.

The hospital is not a final resting place and should not be regarded, therefore, as a place of last resort. It is a medical resource like any other and can be used flexibly to meet the needs of a particular patient. In contrast to the schizophrenic, the manic is not likely to suffer the long-term effects of chronic institutionalization. He can come in one day and be home on pass the next day if that seems appropriate. He can come in over a weekend for a rest, or he can stay for a month or longer until he is ready to return home.

THE MANAGEMENT OF THE ACUTE MANIC STATE

The Administration of Drugs

A number of drugs have found a place in the treatment of mania. Among them are the sedatives and the major tranquilizers. These medications are helpful in treating agitation from whatever cause. They permit the patient to sleep and be relatively calm. It is not possible to communicate effectively with someone who is skipping up and down the ward or singing at the top of his lungs; and so these agents, which allow the patient to sit quietly for a time, allow him also to come into meaningful, therapeutic contact with others. The most important drug in the treatment of mania, however, is lithium, a simple chemical found in varying amounts in ordinary drinking water. About four out of five patients who are in an acute manic state respond to lithium within a period of one to two weeks; if they continue to take it subsequently, they are much less likely to have further manic attacks. They are less vulnerable also to an attack of depression, or to those less severe mood swings that ordinarily might not provoke hospitalization but that untreated might nevertheless prevent working well or functioning well in other capacities.

There is a difficulty in the use of lithium which illustrates why drugs must be given always under close medical supervision. The difference between the therapeutic dose and the toxic dose is very small—in contrast to some other agents, such as penicillin and vitamin C, whose toxic dosage, if there is one, is exceedingly high. If the amount of lithium in the blood drops below a certain level, it loses effectiveness; if that amount is only twice or three times what it should be, serious side effects appear. Those levels differ from individual to individual, and so each patient must be evaluated and followed carefully. Blood tests are required at regular intervals. There are, as usual, minor side effects even at proper blood levels; but these inconveniences do not weigh very heavily in the scale against the terrible disruption of repeated psychotic episodes. The manic-depressive patient who is controlled well on lithium seems to be normal. He is calm, usually without feeling drugged. He is not emotionally dulled. Like other people he can still feel happiness and sorrow in response to the circumstances of his life.

The Therapeutic Environment

The life of the manic is given over to turmoil, so he cannot be expected to sit still and wait for his medications to take effect. Whether he is in the hospital or at home, a therapeutic milieu must be designed for him that will encourage him to rest and will limit his excesses. If he trusts his therapist and the other people taking care of him, he will acquiesce more or less to these constraints.

He should first of all be watched closely so that he does not—as some patients have—embark on the spur of the moment on a cruise to the Orient or invest in a plan to supply the world's starving children with food from the ocean's sludge ("sludge fudge"), or engage in any of the other outlandish schemes that seem to spring readily to the mind of the manic. He should not during this period of impaired judgment be allowed to begin litigation. Similarly he should not marry, divorce, buy a house, or sell his business. He may be allowed other projects, however, which do not involve the expenditure of money and which cannot backfire. There is no danger in his entering, if he so chooses, into a letter-writing campaign to reform the United Nations or the Catholic Church. Sometimes his myriad interests can be focused onto such harmless projects or, indeed, onto worthwhile projects, although the behavior of the manic is so objectionable that he is not likely to advance any cause he espouses.

The manic patient seems to do best in an environment that will at the same time tolerate yet discourage excessive physical activity. Since he is sensitive to bright lights and noise, he should have a quiet room in a quiet setting, if possible; but he cannot usually be locked into it without angering him and increasing his agitation. And yet if he is entirely out of control, there may be no alternative to secluding him. He may be allowed to take frequent walks and to exercise, but not to the point of exhaustion. The more fatigued he becomes, the more he feels the need to drive himself further. He must be told when to sleep and eat. If he becomes physically sick, somehow he must be encouraged to stay in bed. As far as possible he must be prevented from antagonizing other people, for otherwise inevitably they will strike back at him, either physically or through ridicule. Underneath the bravado of the manic is often a sense of failure; being rejected and held in contempt can only worsen such feelings.

Psychotherapy

Psychotherapy has only limited effectiveness during the acute phase of a mania, as it does during an acute depression, and for the same reason: the patient is too preoccupied with his own thoughts to pay attention to anyone else. The manic is in addition too arrogant to listen to anyone, certainly not to someone who is pointing out to him deficiencies in his judgment and telling him what he should and particularly what he should not do. The manic is more likely to point out the therapist's own incapacities and then make frank recommendations to him for self-improvement. Nevertheless the therapist can talk, to some extent at least, to the person who is hiding beneath all of this bluster. One of the presumptions of the psychotherapeutic process is that someone who is behaving irrationally can be appealed to in rational terms—that the truth offered up dispassionately carries with it some measure of conviction.

The manic patient becomes angry every time he is contradicted and every time his wishes are frustrated, and so the therapist need not rush to set himself in opposition; but he will be forced inevitably into that situation from time to time, and he must not cater to his patient's whims out of the desire to avoid a row. Often the manic patient needs guidance, however unwelcome, in order to get successfully through the day.

The goals of psychotherapy during this difficult period are modest. The therapist should tolerate, if he can, his patient's constant ranting, for it serves a purpose. When feelings are expressed in words, they are less likely to be expressed in actions that may be inappropriate. The patient is better off talking about his urge to punch his neighbor or his urge to grab the head nurse than actually punching him or grabbing her. In time he may be able to discuss those feelings that seem most painful to him, namely his feelings of sadness.

Because the manic races from one place to another and from one endeavor to another, he cannot be engaged successfully in conversation usually for more than fifteen or twenty minutes at any one time; and so a psychotherapy session can last no longer. During these sessions, which should be frequent if short, attempts are made to keep the patient talking about one subject at a time. He is so distractible, though, it seems sometimes like trying to catch the wind.

THE MANAGEMENT OF THE RESOLVING MANIA AND THE PERIOD OF REMISSION

Much more can be accomplished once the acute phase of mania has begun to subside. The patient is able then to participate in various treatment modalities, including occupational and recreational therapy. Even group psychotherapy may be possible, although ordinarily someone who is manic is likely to be overstimulated by numbers of people. Sessions of individual therapy can last longer, and as a result the relationship between the patient and his therapist becomes more secure. As the manic becomes less impulsive, his therapist becomes less a controlling person and more a collaborator, helping him to organize his own life and fulfill his own purposes.

An attack of mania may not simply diminish and then disappear, but may terminate instead in a depression. The patient is so troublesome during his manic phase that his family and therapist are all likely to breathe a sigh of relief when he becomes depressed, but then that new condition must be treated. Such a person may feel particular chagrin over his previous extreme behavior while he was manic. Often someone who is loud and seductive or outright obscene while in a manic state may be prim and proper all the rest of the time.

Psychotherapy by itself cannot prevent recurrent psychotic episodes in patients with manic-depressive illness. Someone who is manic will almost certainly recover from that attack, but anyone who has had such an attack is likely to have another. Long-term management, therefore, is directed at discovering these episodes when they first begin in order to minimize the disruption they cause to the patient's life. As in the treatment of all of the relapsing psychoses, the patient's family and therapist must act in close concert, but the burden of the patient's care will fall over the years most heavily on his family.

THE ROLE OF THE FAMILY

A person who is manic from time to time also is usually depressed intermittently, and so his family alternates between concern over his reckless enthusiasm and over his despair. Both states of mind tend to set him apart, for although the manic is intrusive rather than withdrawn, he is so objectionable in manner that he is intolerable to others. The family must put up with him when no one else can. It is no easy task. He is insulting, rude, and demanding. He changes family routines at whim. He may decide that everyone should stay up late at night and get up early in the morning as well. He may show a change in sexual appetite, which although not necessarily in an undesirable direction is at least unsettling to his spouse. He may drink too much and become an embarrassment on that account. Finally he is dangerous to his family and frightening to them because of his inclination to spend money carelessly. They must put up with him anyway for the sake of the person he is when he is well. Very often when he is not psychotic, he is kind and considerate. Considering that the manic-depressive person may be psychotic repeatedly during the course of his life, he usually does remarkably well the rest of the time. Often he is a creative person. He may accomplish useful work and make large sums of money. He may live an effective life by any standard.

But the toll of a manic-depressive illness in a family is heavy. The divorce rate is high. The rate of other members in the family developing an affective illness is also high, whether from the stress of circumstance or for genetic reasons. And suicide among them is not uncommon. Therefore they must care for each other as well as for the person who is acutely manic.

It is difficult, but very important, for the patient's family to recognize when he is becoming ill. He may move abruptly from his usual self into a manic state, but at other times that change may be subtle. He may sleep less or eat more at such times, or he may show some characteristic behavior. One such man always expressed intense interest in the stock market when he was becoming sick. The manic attacks of another patient, a woman, were always heralded by her purchasing colorful dresses, two or three at a time. Some individuals give sign of their mania by unfolding elaborate schemes to make money or to advance various causes. The logic or illogic of these ventures is not always immediately apparent. A clue to the state of mind of the person making such a proposal is his response to criticism. If he becomes irascible at being contradicted, it means probably that he is becoming manic. Otherwise such proposals should not be dismissed out of hand even when put forward by someone with a history of mania. Indeed the mental hygiene movement itself was conceived and carried forward by such a man.* And after all, most of the truly great enterprises throughout history struck someone or other at the time as grandiose.

Once it is clear, however, that someone is indeed becoming manic, he must be treated immediately and vigorously. Certainly he should be given appropriate medication in sufficient amounts, and he should be protected against himself in all the ways mentioned above.

It would be strange if someone who had lived through the terrible experience of mania should willingly choose to become manic again; as a matter of fact, no one ever does. What does happen, however, is that a person who has been manic but is currently depressed searches for some portion of the exhilaration he felt during that previous time. If he feels tired, he may remember the inexhaustible energy he felt previously and forget a little the restless discontent that went with it. He may remember and long for some feeling of exuberance and joy and perhaps sexual excitement, and so he may try to recapture those feelings—by the simple device of refusing his medicine. Yet if he stops taking lithium, the chances of his becoming psychotic again are eight to ten times greater than they would be otherwise.

The patient's family should encourage him to keep taking his medicine, and they usually do. Whatever fun it is for the patient to be a little manic, it is no fun at all for them. They must have his trust, though, for he will not accede to their

---

* Clifford Beers, who wrote *A Mind That Found Itself* in 1908.

judgment unless he feels they have his well-being in mind and are not concerned only with keeping him quiet. Yet it is true certainly that the family of a manic person appreciate him especially when he is quiet.

8 THE DYING PATIENT

DEATH is universal, a fact of everyone's life—not so much one's own death, which is projected psychologically into some unthinkable, indefinite future, but rather the death of others, of the people who are close by. Usually as early as childhood a person experiences the death of a grandparent or some other aged member of the family. Upon growing older he inevitably lives through the death of other relatives, perhaps parents, then as he grows even older, through the death of still others whom he has loved and to whom he has committed himself. Ultimately if he lives long enough, he survives the death, one after another, of brothers and sisters, of most of his friends, of his spouse, and sometimes—perhaps most painful of all—even of his children. Death is a familiar, banal event; yet because it is so purposeless from the point of view of the individual human being, it seems strange and mysterious somehow, even unnatural.

Perhaps it is that sense of strangeness that makes the fact of death hard to accept or to believe in, sometimes even for a physician. Sometimes when a patient of his has expired, he hestitates nevertheless to declare that person dead—for that pronouncement makes him dead irrevocably. The thought of death is abhorrent. So in order to be certain the doctor examines his patient once again. And it may seem to him then that that person for whom he still cares still breathes faintly and hesitantly, and seems still to have a distant pulse. And it may seem to him that he can distinguish an almost imperceptible heartbeat through the stethoscope, because he seeks it so attentively. Yet surely that person is dead.

If the fact of death is hard to determine, its meaning is even more elusive. In a way it has no meaning, for death is arbitrary. Like most of life it is decided by random circumstance that takes no consideration of anyone's wishes or requirements. Sudden death seems even more capricious. All it is, is an ending. But when death takes place over a period of time, it does have significance to the person who is dying and to those others who share his life and who care for him. The time of dying is a special time of life. In order for a person to die successfully—in peace and with some sense of the meaning of his life—he must achieve certain purposes. He must remember and understand his past. He must be able to plan for the future—for there continues always to be a future, for his family or for his work perhaps. He must say good-bye to the people who matter to him. It is a time of drawing away, and yet also a time of drawing close, since the facade that people interpose between each other tends to fall away during these final moments. For that reason, dying is an intimate experience. The person who undergoes this last, most lonely experience must have someone with whom to share it. For some this final time of life must be a time of growing up once and for all. Death is probably always sad and painful to some extent, but for those who come to accept themselves as they really are, there are some days of grace and contentment.

However, there are *disturbances of dying* in which the meaning of death is lost or perverted, with the result that the natural melancholy of death develops into an overt depression or into some other less precise kind of emotional distress; these disturbances, like any other kind of emotional disturbance, require treatment.

Because of the great variability among human beings, no one person can be presented as a typical example of the way someone lives, or dies. But the following report does illustrate a number of the common, if not typical, problems unfortunately associated with the care of a dying patient.

Mr. L. was a handsome robust man who was fifty-two years old when he first became ill. He was then, as he liked to say, "very vigorous," but he had been a vigorous man all his life. He had started his own plumbing business twenty years before and as a result had made a considerable amount of money. He was successful also in community affairs. He had been elected repeatedly an officer of various fraternal organizations, and he had been a scout leader. He was a competent carpenter in addition to being a plumber. He enjoyed working with his hands and had in fact built almost single-handedly the house in which he, his wife, and his two sons had lived most of their lives. He seemed, in short, to be an unusually competent person.

The first symptom of his illness was a vague, cramping abdominal pain, which he dismissed cheerfully as a consequence of his wife's "rotten cooking." However during the following few weeks, his pain became worse. He vomited occasionally and lost weight. Finally at the urging of his family he visited a doctor. He was examined and underwent a full battery of laboratory tests including X-ray examinations. Almost immediately thereafter, on his physician's strident recommendation, an operation was performed, at which time he was found to have cancer. Following this surgical procedure, the patient was informed that he had a "benign growth" which had been removed successfully. His family, however, was told the truth: that the growth was malignant and very likely to recur.

Mr. L. recovered slowly from his operation, apparently without complication. Within a few weeks he had returned home and almost at once he returned to work. Not long afterward, though, he developed a sudden attack of stomach pain and vomiting. He was taken to the hospital in an ambulance. After further X-ray and blood studies he was operated on once again, for acute intestinal obstruction. He was never to recover fully. Over the next five months Mr. L. died slowly and painfully. His pain was not only physical but emotional. And unfortunately the pain was a consequence not only of the inevitable circumstances of dying and death, but also of mismanagement.

Mr. L. spent those months entirely in the hospital under the care of a handful of unusually well-trained physicians and nurses; nevertheless the care he received from them was not adequate to his needs, in part because his relationship with them was poor. They regarded him as uncooperative. After his death they remembered him as a difficult patient who either wanted more medicine or less, but never what was prescribed for him. Similarly he either wanted the staff around his bed tending to him constantly, or he never wanted to see them at all. He objected to all of the rules of the ward. He objected to the limitations on visiting hours. He never wanted to go to bed on time. He complained about having nothing to do. He found fault with the other patients. He rejected medical procedures that were explained to him as essential for his survival. Finally he threatened to sign out of the hospital against medical advice. In short he was considered a troublemaker. Reportedly, a week before he died, he even insulted the priest.

A few weeks after Mr. L. died, his family was asked to describe those last few months of his life. Their account was different, of course, from that of the hospital staff, perhaps because they were more personally involved and to that extent less objective. They were not concerned with the smooth running of the hospital, but rather with the suffering and wasting away of someone whom they loved. And they were affected also by their own terrible sense of impending loss. Mrs. L. summed up the feelings of her family:

"When the doctors told us he had cancer, we couldn't believe it. He always was such a strong person. We didn't know how to behave toward him. I made sure no one in the family told him how sick he really was, since we wanted to make his last days peaceful. But he never let up. He wanted to go back to work, and when that was impossible, he wanted me to bring accounts of the business to the hospital so he could work on them there. He even wanted us to bring his carpentry to the hospital. But I told him to stop worrying and stop working for once in his life. . . . He suffered terribly from pain, and he would get angry. Sometimes he talked about dying, but I always tried to cheer him up. I wouldn't let him give up. Still, after a while, there was nothing to say. . . . It was terrible to see him thinner and thinner, even though he was fed with all those tubes in his arms and in his nose. I felt responsible somehow, but I know we did everything we could, even at the end, to keep him alive."

Because Mr. L. was such a difficult patient, a psychiatrist was called to examine him. Mr. L.'s following remarks are drawn from that interview, which took place two weeks before he died:

"In the first place, I'm not going to talk to you if you're going to give me bullshit about having a positive attitude. I know I have cancer and I know I'm dying; even if no one will admit it. And if you're here to talk me into more X rays, or taking another bunch of experimental drugs—forget it. And I'm not letting anyone stick another tube into me."*

* At that time he had in place a nasal-gastric tube to prevent intestinal obstruction, a "cut-down" into a leg vein to maintain fluid balance, and an in-dwelling urinary

He went on to register a long list of complaints. About the staff: "I have so many doctors I don't know which one is in charge. They look in, they say hello, then they slink away. They won't tell me what's going on. At first they wouldn't give me enough pain medicine. They were afraid I was going to become an addict. Now they give me so much, I'm dopey all the time. The nurses never come when you need them. They make believe I'm not here. Otherwise they fuss all the time and they never leave me alone."

About the hospital: "I suppose I first knew I was dying when they put me on this ward full of dying people. It's a terrible feeling to see one roommate after another die. When someone dies, they tie up a little cord around his big toe with his name and address on it, as if they're going to mail his body home. . . . Of course, I can't do anything here. I can't smoke. I can't read at night because they turn out the light. Certainly I can't do anything useful. . . . For the first couple of months they wouldn't let my grandchildren visit, until I threatened to sign out of the hospital. I see them for only a few minutes. Each time I wonder if that's the last time I'll ever see them."

About his family: "I know they're trying to help me, but they don't understand what I feel or want. I wanted to go over the books of the business with my son. After all, he's going to have to run the business after I'm dead, but my wife refused. She pretends I'm going to get better, and I go along so I won't upset her. But I'm worried about what will happen to them after I'm gone. Since we can't talk about that, we just sit around and don't talk about anything. I can see that they don't even want to visit sometimes. But that's all right."

About things in general: "You know, it's funny, I'm an atheist and I don't believe in anything, but I worry about

catheter to measure urinary output. Under active consideration was a plan to insert an additional tube directly into the subclavian vein in his neck in order to more adequately meet his nutritional needs.

what's going to happen to my body after I die. So I told that to one of the doctors, and he sent me a priest. I couldn't believe it; I haven't seen a priest since I was ten. I had to tell the fellow to leave a dozen times before he would go. I wanted to finish a ship model for my grandson, but they wouldn't let me, and now I'm tired. . . . I want to go home to die, but they won't let me. They want to save my life when there is no life left to save. Each day I spend here costs my family money. Each time they X-ray me, that's that much less money I can leave to my family. . . . I shouldn't say I'm dying now because I died five months ago when I came into this place, for all intents and purposes."

Dying is the most natural condition; it should not be so terrible. Mr. L. would not have died so unhappily if the people who loved him and those who cared for him had not interfered, however inadvertently, with the process of healing that is simultaneous to and, indeed, part of the process of dying. Even during this period of turmoil, those who will be survivors begin to recover from their loss and hurt. And the person who will die is also healed, in a way; for he too accommodates himself slowly to that same loss—if he is permitted to do so. It is not a loss of life per se, but rather the dissolution of emotional attachments. It is the loss of everything and everyone who has mattered to him.

Clinicians have noted that that accommodation takes place in stages through which the individual must travel at his own pace. When he first realizes that he is going to die, he may feel only shock. He refuses to admit, even to himself, that that inconceivable circumstance is true, that sometime soon he will truly no longer be alive. He may ignore his physical condition or attribute his symptoms to some minor illness. He may seem cheerful. He searches out newspaper accounts of medical breakthroughs that have been found to cure his precise complaints. But sooner or later he expresses other feelings. He becomes angry at the unfairness of his illness. Why should he need to die when others who are older or less deserving—or less able to enjoy life—continue on? He blames his physicians for not helping him. He scolds everyone. But as time goes on and as he becomes sicker still, he becomes more tractable. Rather than arguing with his physicians, he bargains with them, and with God, for just a little more time, time enough to see the children graduate, or simply time enough to go on one last vacation. And then finally he draws away from the world. He may seem tired and worn out, or he may become overtly depressed; but last of all, he becomes resigned. He comes to accept the inevitability of that which happens inevitably to everyone—death.

Sometimes someone dies prematurely, before he has come to terms with the fact of his dying. Then he may spend his last weeks and days still railing at the world and at his destiny, or he may deny to the very end of his life the possibility of dying. He may die frightened or in a state of depression. Yet certainly there are many people who die at peace.

Mr. L. suffered more than necessary during the last few months of his life for two principal reasons: the people around him would not, or could not, accept the fact that he was dying; and second, they would not accept him for himself. They treated him impersonally, as a case of cancer, when they should have considered him as a particular individual with his own personality—his own attachments, interests, ambitions, and needs.

Although he was obviously going to die very soon, he was kept alive a few weeks longer, *against his wishes,* by undergoing medical procedures that were very expensive and that only increased his pain and discomfort.

Because no one would concede to him that he was going to die, he was prevented from saying good-bye to his family. And because he could not discuss with them that fact, which was foremost in all of their minds, they could find nothing at all to talk about.

The doctors and nurses in charge of his care felt guilty about their inability to save him, and so they avoided him—by placing him on a ward with other hopeless cases and by dividing their responsibility so that no one person needed to spend much time with him. And so much of the time he was alone.

Although he had always been an independent person, he was not allowed to make ordinary decisions about his life. He was managed, often arbitrarily, by his physicians, by hospital staff, and by his wife. His eating, sleeping, elimination, and all of his daily activities were determined for him by others, as if he were a child.

Finally because his life was in danger, his identity—his sense of himself—was threatened profoundly; and at just that precisely wrong time, he was prevented from engaging in activities that were the foundation of his self-esteem and self-image. His dedication to his business and its success, his satisfaction at being able to work with his hands, and, most important, his concern over his family's future were all ignored. His religious convictions were slighted. As the result his values and his respect for himself were undermined. Everything he had always been was made out to be unimportant.

The treatment of the dying patient is directed at making the remainder of his life as comfortable and, even more important, as fulfilling as possible.

Necessary to that purpose, and of importance in its own right, is the emotional well-being of the patient's family. Invariably they find it difficult at such a time to maintain their own equilibrium, and yet this care requires their best resources. Indeed, taking care of a dying person is difficult and stressful for anyone, including medical and nursing staff. Yet the experience of providing such care is often enriching, even ennobling.

THE ROLE OF THE THERAPIST

Everyone with whom the dying patient comes in contact is cast in the role of therapist. Each one of them has the potential to make him feel either somewhat better or somewhat worse. In order to be helpful, however, the therapist, whoever he is, must know the patient, must know about his illness, and must know himself. Also he should know life well enough not to be afraid of death.

Character is the principal determinant of the way someone lives and ultimately dies. His behavior during the time of his dying grows naturally out of everything that has gone before; at the end of his life, he is still the same person he has always been. Therefore the same things matter to him. For that reason he should be allowed to engage in his usual pursuits, within the limits of his physical strength. He should work a little, if he can and if he wants to. He should continue his hobbies. Certainly he should read if he wants to, even into the small hours of the night. In short, he can use his energies, even dissipate his energies, just as he chooses.

His particular needs must be met, not his needs as someone would expect them to be, but as they really are—as he expresses them. Since many people find religion comforting, he should have the opportunity for pastoral counseling and for prayer; if he does not want to avail himself of that opportunity, he should be left alone.

The patient's concerns must be addressed, and these too may not be what someone would anticipate. The typical patient is likely, of course, to worry about how painful or uncomfortable the last days of his life will be. Probably he will worry also about his family and about their future. He may even worry about their worrying about him. In addition to these realistic and perhaps inevitable concerns, some patients have fears that are really outgrowths of neurotic conflict.

Death may suggest something special to them, the fantasy, perhaps, of lying helpless underground, or the related fantasy of physical dismemberment or dissolution. Usually some device can be found to reassure such individuals, even though there is no time to analyze their underlying emotional conflicts.

Often the fear of death that some patients express is recognized on close examination to be a different fear altogether, such as the fear of separation and loneliness, the fear of loss of control, or the fear of pain, disfigurement, or failure. These patients, too, can be reassured by addressing their real fears. For example, they should know that they will not be abandoned. No matter how sick they become, someone will be there to take care of them. And they should be led to understand that however severe their pain becomes, they will be given, *promptly*, enough medication to relieve it. Also they should be assured that however sick they may become, attention will be given to their physical appearance, so that they always look presentable. Finally someone must find time to speak with them about their lives so that the fact that they have not accomplished everything that they set out to do when they were children is not construed by them as a failure.

Dying patients must be cared for even if they cannot be cured, and their treatment varies, depending upon their illness. Some conditions are more painful than others. Some are more enervating or more incapacitating. Some affect the special senses, such as sight or hearing, and consequently cause particular distress. Each illness represents a special problem in management which must be solved in order that the patient not be distracted from the remainder of his life by constant physical suffering.

If it has become plain that he will die from his illness, the goal of medical management should be to make him as comfortable as possible for as long as possible. However, heroic attempts to delay the final moment of death should be avoided, for they are invariably distressing to the patient and his family. They are a mockery of the medical purpose, which is to prolong life, not death. For similar reasons a conscious effort should be made to spare the patient the potentially endless series of medical and laboratory procedures that seem to spring readily to the medical mind and that, if allowed to intrude into each day, can prevent anyone, however wise and mature, from dying in peace.

Any seriously ill person should be informed about his condition, and the dying patient is no exception. In this connection the question is usually raised about whether or not someone should be told that he is going to die. The answer, of course, is that he should be told what he wants to know. Many patients reveal in their questions, or in their lack of questions, that they do not want to contemplate the possibility of dying. No purpose is served then by denying them that escape. Consequently no unhappy information should be volunteered to them, although, again, whatever questions they ask should be answered. When patients really want to know about their condition, then surely they should be told—not how much longer they have to live, for that period of time is never predictable, but rather the likely course that their illness will take. Even bad news is a relief sometimes from the anguish of uncertainty. The fact is, however, that most patients who are so desperately ill know well enough that they are dying. What each person needs to know, and be reminded of, is that there is hope for him, as indeed there is always hope, and that in any case he will be cared for and attended to the very end.

The therapist is important to the patient because of who he is rather than what he says or does: it is the relationship between them that matters. The therapist must be able to tolerate the painful intimacy that dying patients share in even their brief encounters. He must be compassionate and understanding, and steadfast. He must himself have made peace with death, the death of those close to him and his own death yet to come. And he must have found meaning in life.

THE ROLE OF THE FAMILY

The family must serve as therapist to the dying person, often as the only therapist, since too often no one else is willing to tend to his emotional needs. They must have all the virtues of the therapist and, in addition, courage. If at this critical moment they are not afraid, he will feel less frightened. But they should not ply him with false optimism or in some other way treat him like a child. They should be patient. If he becomes irritable or unreasonable, they should not become personally offended. The important task that they can do for him better than anyone else can is simply to be with him. For that reason consideration should be given when possible to removing the dying patient home, where his treatment can be continued. He is usually more comfortable there and less alone. He can be with the members of his family who will live after him, and consequently see more clearly the continuity of his own life with theirs. If he finally chooses to be by himself, that wish too is usually easier to satisfy at home than at the hospital.

Of course the family must tend also to themselves. They cannot expend all of their energies indefinitely in the care of one of them who is dying. They should have time off occasionally from sitting with the patient. They should be able to enjoy themselves then without feeling guilty. Certainly they cannot stay away from work or from school for any length of time. Also they should try to be with each other. They will be comforted by sharing their feelings of grief, for death is lonely even to those who survive. Finally they should make proper plans for their future, especially their financial future, so that they—and the patient, who is committed to them—can feel secure.

MOURNING

The process of mourning begins long before the moment of death itself. It begins when the family realizes for the first time that the person who is sick is actually going to die. Like the process of dying, mourning takes place in stages that merge into each other. The dying person is let go of by those who love him only a little bit at a time. At first they are shocked and disbelieving. However bluntly the doctor has spoken to them, they search his remarks for the loophole that would give them reason to hope. They ask for consultations with other physicians. Although unversed in medicine, they may suggest medical treatments of one sort or another. Later they may become angry at the doctor or indeed at the patient himself. The doctor should have been more alert to the significance of the patient's symptoms. Or the patient should have taken care of himself better. Or someone else—his wife, perhaps, or his mother—should have seen to it that he took care of himself. It seems that no one ever dies a natural death; someone is always to blame. Often the family, especially the children in the family, feel rejected by the dying person. It is as if he were dying on purpose. Sometimes God is blamed.

Even after someone has died, he has not vanished entirely. His presence seems to linger on. Children in particular cannot conceive of the permanence of death, no matter what they are told. It is outside their experience. And so to them the dead person is simply away for a while. But even adults grasp the reality of death slowly. At first they think of the dead person constantly and painfully. They resurrect him in their dreams, sometimes night after night. Only after a while do they find room in their thoughts for other people. Yet as time goes on, their sense of loss becomes less terrible. They look for and find some reason to think that what happened was for the best. They think of the deceased less and less frequently, and finally they are healed. Even then the memory of that person, if he was especially important—a spouse, perhaps, or a parent— fades slowly. He seems to be present still, somewhere nearby.

Sometimes the work of mourning does not go smoothly. Sometimes death is so terrible, so poignant, that it is unacceptable. And sometimes the survivors are so unprepared emotionally for their loss that they cannot grieve properly. They become vulnerable then to depression or to some other pathological emotional reaction. These can become so severe that they require formal psychiatric intervention. To an extent, however, such conditions can be prevented by paying proper attention to the family's emotional needs during the period of mourning, including the time before the patient dies.

Most religions set rules governing the management of death and the way people are supposed to behave when someone dies. These practices serve to facilitate the healthy process of mourning. They vary from one religion to another, but include customarily a time for quiet and the sharing of feelings of sadness among the bereaved family and friends. The prescribed rituals of the funeral and of burial are also important, since they help to bring home to everyone the fact of death. Usually these customs should be observed by the whole family, including the children—for it is a time for gathering together.

There is no way to put a good face on death; it is the essential tragedy of life. At the end of success or failure, at the end of all struggle, there is always death. But there is a proper way to die. Even dying, someone can make the best of life. If he cannot work, still he can accomplish some things. He can arrange his affairs. He can write to people and continue to influence them. If he is in the hospital, often he can be helpful and comforting to other patients. Even dying, he can still love. He can still take pleasure from the company of friends and from simple occupations, such as looking out of a window or reading a book. There is still time to be curious and to learn. And there is still satisfaction in planning for the future for his family. Leaving life is less painful for someone when his emotional investment is not exclusively in himself, but rather in his children who live on after him, or in ideals or goals that continue to be meaningful even after he has gone. In short, the things that have always mattered still matter. The very end of life is of a piece with what has gone before. In order for someone to die with grace, he must be allowed to express himself, even in that last portion of life, as the person he has always been.

AFTERWORD

PSYCHIATRISTS like to think that they approach their patients objectively, with no preconceived opinions about the way life ought to be lived; but the fact is that they are not unbiased. Their judgment, like that of everyone else, is influenced by the sum of their previous experiences; since those experiences are very different from one psychiatrist to the next, their outlook upon the world is also different. Each among them has his own values—indeed, his own prejudices about the meaning and purpose of life. These ideas, which may be unconscious and unarticulated, are conveyed nevertheless in one way or another to patients, invariably affecting them and sometimes completely determining their response to psychotherapy. Consequently such ideas and attitudes are important. Reading through these chapters, I recognize my own point of view written out between the lines. I think, to be fair, I should not close this book without first trying to state that vague ideology, as far as I am aware of it, as openly and explicitly as I can.

Life—or even one's point of view toward it—is, however, too large a topic to comment upon simply and at the same time sensibly. The circumstances of life are always diverse, and people themselves are complex beyond all measure. Psychiatrist or not, I have not understood people so well that I can explain them. More important, I have no formula to recommend by which everyone, or indeed anyone, can find happiness. But I think that life has meaning. And I know that there are ways of living happily, for there are happy people.

People who are happy tend to resemble each other, first of all in the conventional sense that they are likely to be married and have children, and have friends, and be employed—either at earning a living or at maintaining a home, and often at both. But also their attitudes toward life are similar. Almost always they are committed—sometimes to a person or to a cause, but always to the process of living itself. They are from time to time joyful and passionate, thoughtful at times and given over to action at other times. They are deeply involved in the everyday business of their lives. Their relationships with others are marked by a spirit of sharing and mutual concern. They love. Certainly there are exceptions to these general rules. For example a man can be a bachelor and still be happy. A woman can be childless and nevertheless feel content and fulfilled. Similarly someone may be active to the exclusion of ever stopping to think critically about himself, or conversely he may be contemplative to an extreme; and in either case still he may be happy. But nevertheless I think in each of these examples that particular person has missed some portion of life. Intentionally or not he has sacrificed something important. I know this is a conventional and banal idea: that certain experiences, including friendship, marriage, parenthood, work, and so on, are on balance good experiences and central to a successful life. But still it seems to me to be true.

Emotional illness, of course, makes all of these experiences less likely to occur and also less likely to be satisfactory if they do occur. Indeed such conditions tend to interfere with much of what makes life exciting and worthwhile. They impair functioning, and they make people miserable in the bargain. Treatment, therefore, and psychotherapy in particular, may be construed as a strategy to relieve that suffering and compensate for those impairments of functioning brought on by these illnesses. It is a rational, pragmatic attempt to be helpful. It is not, of course, an attempt to marry off the bachelor or make pregnant the woman who has not borne children. It is not, or should not be, an attempt to win the patient over to the therapist's style of living. Rather, psychotherapy is a systematic effort to enlarge the patient's options, so that he can venture away from his stereotyped behavior and choose for himself a better way of living.

Perhaps it is that vision of man as mutable that is the central thesis, the fundamental prejudice, to which I and, I think, every psychotherapist hold. I believe that people can change and grow, even those who have been crippled emotionally. With help, patients and people in general can comprehend and take charge of their lives. It is a faith in the rational aspects of man; it is a belief also in the wholly irrational but not unreasonable inclination of man to prefer pleasure to pain, and happiness to discontent. It seems to me, finally, that people are capable of dealing more or less effectively with all of the problems of life so that, with some good fortune, they may grasp life with a sense of adventure and exhilaration, and they may fulfill themselves.

SELECTED REFERENCES AND RECOMMENDED READING

GENERAL READING

Ackerman, N. *The Psychodynamics of Family Life*. New York: Basic Books, 1958.

Bird, Brian. *Talking with Patients*. Philadelphia: J. B. Lippincott, 1973.

Bridges, P. K. *Psychiatric Emergencies: Diagnosis and Management*. Springfield, Ill.: Charles C. Thomas, 1971.

Burch, Claire. *Stranger in the Family: A Guide to Living with the Emotionally Disturbed*. New York: Bobbs Merrill, 1972.

Erikson, E. *Childhood and Society*. New York: W. W. Norton, 1963.

Frank, J. D. "Psychotherapy: The Restoration of Morale." *American Journal of Psychiatry*, Vol. 131 (1974), pp. 271–74.

Freedman, A., and H. Kaplan, eds. *Comprehensive Textbook of Psychiatry*. (Second edition) Baltimore: Williams and Wilkins, 1975.

Goldberg, Harold L. "Home Treatment." *Psychiatric Annals*, Vol. 3, No. 6 (June 1973), pp. 59–61.

Herskowitz, Ralph G. "Crisis Theory: A Formulation." *Psychiatric Annals*, Vol. 3, No. 12 (Dec. 1973), pp. 33–47.

Howells, J. G. *The Theory and Practice of Family Psychiatry*. New York: Brunner/Mazel, 1971.

Langsley, D. G., and D. M. Kaplan. *The Treatment of Families in Crisis*. New York: Grune & Stratton, 1968.

Paul, G. L., and R. J. Lentz. *Psychological Treatment of Chronic Mental Pa-*

tients: Milieu vs. Social-Learning Programs. Cambridge: Harvard University Press, 1977.

Turek, I. S., and E. L. Ansel. "Prevention of Chronicity: An Overview." *Psychiatric Annals*, Vol. 8, No. 11 (Nov. 1978), pp. 12–32.

Wolberg, L. R. *The Technique of Psychotherapy.* New York: Grune & Stratton, 1977.

SUICIDE AND VIOLENCE

Beall, Lynnette. "The Dynamics of Suicide: A Review of the Literature, 1897–1965." *Reflections*, Vol. 5, No. 5 (1970), pp. 12–38.

Duncan, James W., and Glen Duncan. "Murder in the Family: A Study of Some Homicidal Adolescents." *American Journal of Psychiatry*, Vol. 127, No. 11 (May 1971), pp. 1498–1502.

Farberow, N. L., and E. S. Shneidman. *The Cry for Help.* New York: McGraw-Hill, 1961.

Farberow, Dr. N. L., and P. Sainsbury, eds. *Prevention of Suicide.* World Health Organization Public Health Papers #35. Geneva.

Hendin, H. *Black Suicide.* New York: Basic Books, 1969.

———. *Suicide and Scandinavia.* New York: Grune & Stratton, 1964.

Kiev, Ari. *The Suicidal Patient: Recognition and Management.* Chicago: Nelson-Hall, 1977.

Lion, John, Denis Madden, and Russell Christopher. "A Violence Clinic: Three Years' Experience." *American Journal of Psychiatry*, Vol. 133, No. 4 (April 1976), pp. 432–35.

MacDonald, J. M. "Homicidal Threats." *American Journal of Psychiatry*, Vol. 124 (1969), pp. 1252–58.

———.* *Homicidal Threats.* Springfield, Ill.: Charles C. Thomas, 1968.

Menninger, K. A. *Man Against Himself.* New York: Harcourt Brace, 1958.

Minkoff, K., and E. Bergman, A. Beck, and R. Beck. "Hopelessness, Depression, and Attempted Suicide." *American Journal of Psychiatry*, Vol. 130, No. 4 (April 1973), pp. 455–59.

Sadoff, R. L., ed. *Violence and Responsibility: The Individual, the Family and Society.* SP Medical and Scientific Books (Englewood Cliffs, N.J.: Spectrum Publications), 1978.

Selkin, J., and A. Braucht. "Home Treatment of Suicidal Persons."

*With a chapter by Margaret Mead

Emergency and Disaster Management, ed. H. Parad, et al. Bowie, Md.: Charles Press, 1976.

Shneidman, Edwin, Norman L. Farberow, and Robert Lithman. *The Psychology of Suicide*. New York: Science House, 1970.

Stone, A. A. "A Syndrome of Serious Suicidal Intent." *Archives of General Psychiatry*, Vol. 3 (1960), pp. 331–39.

Tabachnick, N. "Interpersonal Relationship in Suicidal Attempts: Some Psychodynamic Considerations and Implications for Treatment." *Archives of General Psychiatry*, Vol. 4 (1961), pp. 16–21.

CHILD ABUSE

Anthony, E., and T. Benedek, eds. *Parenthood: Its Psychology and Psychopathology*. Boston: Little, Brown, 1970.

Bourne, R., and E. Newburger, eds. *Critical Perspectives on Child Abuse*. Lexington, Mass.: Lexington Books (D. C. Heath & Co.), 1979.

Fontana, Vincent J. *Somewhere a Child Is Crying*. New York: Mentor Books, 1976.

———. "Violence Begins at Home." *Journal of the American Academy of Child Psychiatry*, Vol. 10 (1971), pp. 336–50.

Green, A. H. "Psychiatric Treatment of Abused Children." *Journal of the American Academy of Child Psychiatry*, Vol. 17, pp. 356–71.

———. "A Psychodynamic Approach to the Study and Treatment of Abusing Parents." *Journal of the American Academy of Child Psychiatry*, Vol. 15 (1976), pp. 414–29.

Green, Arthur, Richard Gaines, and Alice Sandgrund. "Child Abuse: Pathological Syndrome of Family Interaction." *American Journal of Psychiatry*, Vol. 131, No. 8 (Aug. 1974), pp. 882–86.

Helfer, R. E., and C. H. Kempe, eds. *The Battered Child*. (Second edition) Chicago: University of Chicago Press, 1974.

Helfer, R. E., and C. H. Kempe. *Child Abuse and Neglect: The Family and the Community*. Cambridge: Ballinger Pub. Co. (J. B. Lippincott), 1976.

Kempe, C. H., and R. E. Helfer, eds. *Helping the Battered Child and His Family*. Philadelphia: J. B. Lippincott, 1972.

Martin, Harold, ed. *The Abused Child: A Multidisciplinary Approach to Developmental Issues and Treatment*. Cambridge: Ballinger Pub. Co. (J. B. Lippincott), 1976.

Terr, L. C. "A Family Study of Child Abuse." *American Journal of Psychiatry*, Vol. 127, No. 5 (Nov. 1970), pp. 665–71.

SCHIZOPHRENIA

Arieti, S. *Interpretation of Schizophrenia.* New York: Robert Brunner, 1955.

———. "Parents of the Schizophrenic Patient: A Reconsideration." *J. Amer. Acad. Psychoanalysis,* Vol. 5, No. 3 (July 1977), pp. 347–58.

———. *Understanding and Helping the Schizophrenic.* New York: Basic Books, 1979.

Bellak, L. *Schizophrenia: A Review of the Syndrome.* New York: Logos Press, 1958.

Bowen, M., R. Dysinger, et al. "The Role of the Father in Families with a Schizophrenic Patient." *American Journal of Psychiatry,* Vol. 115 (1958), pp. 1017–20.

Brody, Eugene, and Fredrick Redlich. *Psychotherapy with Schizophrenics.* New York: International Universities Press, 1952.

Davis, Anne E., Simon Dinitz, and Benjamin Pasamanick. *Schizophrenics in the New Custodial Community: Five Years After the Experiment.* Columbus: Ohio University Press, 1974.

Frank, J. "The Role of Hope in Psychotherapy." *Int. J. Psychiatry,* Vol. 5 (1968), p. 383.

Friedman, A., et al. *Psychotherapy for the Whole Family.* New York: Springer-Verlag, 1965.

Herz, M. "Prevention of Chronicity in Schizophrenia." *Psychiatric Annals,* Vol. 8, No. 11 (Nov. 1978), p. 8.

Herz, M. I., J. Endicott, and R. L. Spitzer. "Brief vs. Standard Hospitalization: The Families." *American Journal of Psychiatry,* Vol. 133 (1976), pp. 795–801.

Hill, L. *Psychotherapeutic Interventions in Schizophrenia.* Chicago: University of Chicago Press, 1955.

Jackson, D. D. "A Suggestion for the Technical Handling of Paranoid Patients." *Psychiatry,* Vol. 26 (1963), pp. 306–7.

Katz, Philip. "The Therapy of Adolescent Schizophrenia." *American Journal of Psychiatry,* Vol. 127, No. 2 (Aug. 1970), pp. 132–37.

Lidz, T. *The Origin and Treatment of Schizophrenic Disorders.* New York: Basic Books, 1973.

Lidz, T., and S. Fleck. *Schizophrenia and the Family.* New York: International Universities Press, 1965.

Mosher, L. R., A. Z. Menn, and S. M. Mathews. "Soteria: Evaluation of a Home-Based Treatment for Schizophrenia." *Am. J. Orthopsychiatry,* Vol. 45 (1975), pp. 455–67.

Mosher, Loren R., and Samuel Keith. "Research on the Psychosocial Treatment of Schizophrenia: A Summary Report." *American Journal of Psychiatry*, Vol. 136, No. 5 (May 1979), pp. 623–30.

Rosenbaum, C. P. *The Meaning of Madness*. New York: Science House, 1970.

Seeman, M. "Management of Schizophrenic Patients." *Canadian Medical Association Journal*, Vol. 120 (1979), pp. 1097–1104.

Shershow, J., ed. *Schizophrenia: Science and Practice*. Cambridge: Harvard University Press, 1978.

Soher, Sam C., and Howard R. Davis, eds. *The Outpatient Treatment of Schizophrenia*. New York: Grune & Stratton, 1960.

Truax, C., and D. Wargo. "Human Encounters That Change Behavior for the Better or Worse." *American Journal of Psychotherapy*, Vol. 20 (1966), pp. 499–520.

West, L. J., ed. *Treatment of Schizophrenia: Progress and Prospects*. New York: Grune & Stratton, 1976.

Wing, J. K. "The Social Context of Schizophrenia." *American Journal of Psychiatry*, Vol. 135, No. 11 (Nov. 1978), pp. 1333–39.

Wynne, L. C., and M. T. Singer. "Thought Disorder and Family Relations of Schizophrenics, III and IV." *Archives of General Psychiatry*, Vol. 12 (1965), p. 187.

DEPRESSION

Anthony, E. J., and T. Benedek. *Depression and Human Existence*. Boston: Little, Brown, 1975.

Arieti, S. "Psychotherapeutic Approach to Severely Depressed Patients." *American Journal of Psychotherapy*, Vol. 27 (1978), pp. 33–47.

Arieti, S., and J. Bembard. *Severe and Mild Depression: The Psychotherapeutic Approach*. New York: Basic Books, 1978.

Beck, Aaron T. *The Diagnosis and Management of Depression*. Philadelphia: University of Pennsylvania Press, 1973.

Flach, F. *The Secret Strength of Depression*. Philadelphia: J. B. Lippincott, 1974.

Lesse, Stanley, ed. *Masked Depression*. New York: Jason Aronson, 1975.

Mendels, Joseph. *Concepts of Depression*. New York: John Wiley, 1970.

Ostow, Mortimer. *The Psychology of Melancholy*. New York: Harper and Row, 1970.

SENILITY AND DEPRESSION IN THE AGED

Bayne, J. "Management of Confusion in Elderly Persons." *Canadian Medical Association Journal*, Vol. 21 (1978), pp. 139–41.

Bellak, L., and T. B. Karasu, eds. *Geriatric Psychiatry: A Handbook for Psychiatrists and Primary Care Physicians*. New York: Grune & Stratton, 1976.

Braceland, Francis J. "Senescence—The Inside Story." *Psychiatric Annals*, Vol. 2, No. 10 (Oct. 1972), pp. 48–62.

Busse, E. W., and E. Pfeiffer. *Behavior and Adaptation in Late Life*. (Second edition) Boston: Little, Brown, 1977.

Butler, R. N. *Why Survive? Being Old in America*. New York: Harper & Row, 1975.

Butler, R. N., and M. I. Lewis. *Aging and Mental Health, Positive Psychosocial Approaches*. (Second edition) St. Louis: C. V. Mosby Co., 1977.

Gitelson, M. "The Emotional Problems of Elderly People." *Geriatrics*, Vol. 3 (1948), pp. 135–50.

Goldfarb, A., and A. Turner. "Psychotherapy of Aged Persons—Utilization and Effectiveness of Brief Therapy." *American Journal of Psychiatry*, Vol. 109 (1953), pp. 916–21.

Levin, S. "Depression in the Aged: A Study of the Salient External Factors." *Geriatrics*, Vol. 18 (1963), pp. 302–7.

Meerloo, J. A. "Psychotherapy with Elderly People." *Geriatrics*, Vol. 10 (1955), pp. 583–87.

Saperstein, S. "Psychotherapy for Geriatric Patients." *New York State Journal of Medicine*, Vol. 72 (1972), pp. 2743–48.

Swenson, W. M. "The Many Faces of Aging." *Geriatrics*, Vol. 17 (1962), pp. 659–63.

MANIA

Bellak, L. *Manic-Depressive Psychosis and Allied Conditions*. New York: Grune & Stratton, 1968.

Jamison, Kay, and Robert Gerner, Constance Hammen, and Christine Padesky. "Clouds and Silver Linings: Positive Experiences Associates with Primary Affective Disorders." *American Journal of Psychiatry*, Vol. 136 (Feb. 1980), pp. 198–202.

Janowsky, D. S., M. Leff, and R. S. Epstein. "Playing the Manic Game." *Archives of General Psychiatry*, Vol. 22 (1970), pp. 252–61.

Kaplan, Harold I., and Benjamin Sadock. "An Overview of the Major Affective Disorders." *Psychiatric Annals*, Vol. 4, No. 6 (June 1973), pp. 13–52.

Winokur, G., R. J. Clayton, and T. Reich. *Manic-Depressive Illness*. St. Louis: C. V. Mosby Co., 1969.

DEATH AND DYING

Bowers, M. K., E. N. Jackson, J. A. Knight, and L. LeShan. *Counseling the Dying*. New York: Nelson, 1964.

Easson, W. M. *The Dying Child*. Springfield, Ill.: Charles C. Thomas, 1970.

Feifel, H., ed. *The Meaning of Death*. New York: McGraw-Hill, 1959.

Furman, Edna. *A Child's Parent Dies: Studies in Childhood Bereavement*. New Haven: Yale University Press, 1974.

Greenblatt, M. "The Grieving Spouse." *American Journal of Psychiatry*, Vol. 135, No. 1 (Jan. 1978), pp. 43–48.

Hinton, J. M. *Dying*. Baltimore: Penguin Books, 1967.

Jackson, E. N. *Telling a Child About Death*. New York: Channel Press, 1965.

Kastenbaum, Robert, and Ruth Aisenberg. *The Psychology of Death*. New York: Springer, 1972.

Kubler-Ross, E. *On Death and Dying*. New York: Macmillan, 1969.

———. *Questions and Answers on Death and Dying*. New York: Macmillan, 1974.

Lindemann, E. "Symptomatology and Management of Acute Grief." *American Journal of Psychiatry*, Vol. 101 (1944), pp. 141–48.

Pattison, E. M., ed. *The Experience of Dying*. Englewood Cliffs, N.J.: Prentice-Hall, 1977.

Pearson, L., ed. *Death and Dying*. Cleveland: Case Western Reserve University Press, 1969.

Peretz, D., et al. *Death and Grief: Selected Readings*. New York: Health Sciences Publishing Corp., 1977.

Rosenthal, H. R. "Psychotherapy for the Dying." *American Journal of Psychotherapy*, Vol. 11 (1957), pp. 626–33.

Sahler, O., ed. *The Child and Death*. St. Louis: C. V. Mosby Co., 1978.

Saunders, Cicely. *The Care of the Dying*. London: Macmillan, 1959.

COMPLETING THE CIRCLE

Discovering the Fullness of Life After Fifty

Margaret Torrie M.B.E.

This book is about the challenge of the middle years and how it can be met. Too many people feel that life is effectively over when they reach the age of fifty, or when they retire; but in fact life remains full of creative possibilities.

Margaret Torrie, founder-director of the Cruse Organization for the bereaved, examines the mid-life crisis and suggests ways of coming to terms with advancing age and of re-assessing the potential we all have for living a full and rewarding life.

The main purpose of the book is to encourage self-awareness and self-analysis in order, as the author says, 'to find a balance within the true art of living'. Achieving this balance, this realization of our inner resources and how they can be used to react positively and fruitfully with the world, should be the goal of the middle years and may even be the 'pearl of great price for which many men and women long'.